The
Cockatiel

An Owner's Guide To

A HAPPY HEALTHY PET

Howell Book House

Howell Book House
A Simon & Schuster Macmillan Company
1633 Broadway
New York, NY 10019

Library of Congress Cataloging-in-Publication Data
Rach, Julie Ann.
The cockatiel : an owner's guide to a happy, healthy pet /by Julie Ann Rach
    p. cm.
  Includes bibliographical references.
  ISBN: 0-87605-526-9
  1. Cockatiel I. Title
SF473.C6R33   1997
636.6'86563 dc21   97-7624
                                 CIP

Manufactured in the United States of America
10 9 8 7 6 5 4 3 2 1

Series Director: Ariel Cannon
Series Assistant Director: Jennifer Liberts
Book Design: Michele Laseau
Cover Design: Iris Jeromnimon
Illustration: Casey Price
Photography:
  Cover and inset by B. Everett Webb
  Back cover by B. Everett Webb
  Joan Balzarini: 50, 54, 64, 114, 116, 120
  Mary Bloom: 42, 46, 47, 48, 82–83, 87, 92, 96
  Trenna Gordon: 5, 8, 15, 51
  Eric Ilasenko: 7, 9, 13, 20, 43, 44, 49, 57, 84, 89, 107, 113, 115
  Cheryl Primeau: 10, 11, 24, 36, 69, 97, 99
  David Schilling: 34, 78, 85
  B. Everett Webb: 3–4, 6, 12, 16, 17, 18–19, 21, 25, 27, 28, 30, 32, 41, 52, 53, 58, 61,
    66, 91,103, 105, 106, 108, 114, 116
Production Team: John Carroll, Kathleen Caulfield, Michelle Croninger,
  Stephanie Hammett, Stephanie Mohler, Terri Sheehan and Karen Teo

Contents

Welcome
to the World

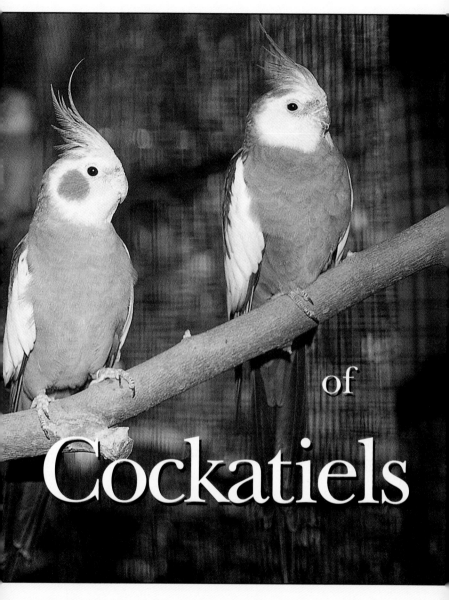

of

Cockatiels

External Features of the Cockatiel

Crown

Nape

Nare

Cere

Mantle

Beak

Breast

Rump

Tail Feathers
(retrices)

chapter 1

About

Cockatiels

Second in popularity only to budgies, cockatiels have charmed many people. Some say it's their small size or affordable price that makes cockatiels so appealing, while others cite their appearance or personalities. Others are captivated by the cockatiel's whistling

abilities, cleanliness and long potential life span. Finally, many bird owners are attracted to the cockatiel's curiosity and adaptability.

In any case, cockatiels can be wonderful pets that reward their owners with years of entertainment and companionship. In return for this love, a cockatiel requires care and attention from his owner.

The Cockatiel's Background

"Although one of the most soberly coloured members of the parrot family, the cockatiel has long been popular among aviculturists by reason of its hardiness, prolificacy and gentle disposition," wrote the noted aviculturist, the Duke of Bedford, in his book *Parrots and Parrot-like Birds* in the early 1950s. The cockatiel

is still popular some forty years later. According to statistics from the American Pet Product Manufacturer Association, about 16 million pet birds are kept in American homes, and 34 percent of them are cockatiels.

The cockatiel originated in Australia, which is home to some fifty parrot species. In its homeland, the cockatiel is sometimes called the quarrion, the weero, the cockatoo parrot or the crested parrot. Small flocks of two to twelve birds gather together to live in Australia's interior, feeding on seedling grasses and other plants. Their habitats can range from open euca-

The first cockatiels were described by naturalists in Australia around 1770.

lyptus savannas to arid grasslands. Cockatiel flocks depend on rainfall for water and, once a steady supply of food and water are available, to establish the start of the breeding season.

In the wild, cockatiels are active during the early morning and the late afternoon. These are the times they usually head toward a water source to drink, being sure to drink and leave quickly rather than become a meal for a passing bird of prey. They spend a good bit of their day on the ground, searching for food, but they are likely to spend midday blending into their surroundings by sitting lengthwise along dead tree branches that are free of foliage.

The cockatiel was first described by naturalists who visited Australia with Captain James Cook in 1770, and the first specimen may have come to the Royal College of Surgeons Museum in England as a result of this trip. The Australian government imposed a ban on exporting all native birds in 1894, so the cockatiels kept in North America and Europe have resulted from domestic breeding efforts in those countries for more than 100 years.

Lots of cockatiels have a distinctive color combination of gray, white and yellow.

Cockatiel or Cockatoo?

Many consider the cockatiel to be the smallest of the cockatoos. Here are some comparisons between cockatiels true parrots and cockatoos. See if you agree with the experts who think the cockatiel is really a tiny cockatoo.

CHARACTERISTICS COCKATIELS SHARE WITH COCKATOOS

- crests
- cockatiel hens and some cockatoos have bars on the undersides of their tail feathers
- male and female birds alternate incubation duties
- cockatiel hens do not feed regurgitated food; both parents feed chicks
- the color combination of gray, white and yellow doesn't occur in true adult parrots but does in cockatoos
- cheek patches occur in cockatiels and some cockatoos

7

- cockatiels and cockatoos both make dramatic sweeping beak movements, followed by holding the head back, when drinking

- cockatiels and cockatoos make similar noises while eating

- first down feathers of the young are yellow. Cockatiels and cockatoos don't shed down feathers, but they turn instead into "powder feathers," which produce a waterproof powder later on.

Cockatiels have tails that are long and narrow with feathers arranged in steps.

- first plumage changes completely after first molt

- both cockatiel and cockatoo chicks remain partially naked before their feathers come in

- cockatiels and most cockatoos don't engage in courtship displays, such as the male feeding the female

- cockatiels and cockatoos show fear in similar ways. Birds crouch low, rock slowly from side to side, hiss, fan their tails and lift the front part of the wings while keeping the wing tips close to the body.

How the Cockatiel Got Its Name

What do you think: Is the cockatiel just a smaller cockatoo? Since experts are still trying to answer the question definitively and since the cockatiel has some anatomical differences from the other seventeen members of the cockatoo family, the cockatiel has been classified into its own genus *Nymphicus* and has its own species name, *hollandicus*. The scientific name, which went through several variations before a naturalist named Wagler settled on its present form in 1832, translates literally to "goddess of New Holland," which is the name Australia was known by in the 1700s and 1800s.

This is a beautiful example of color mutation.

The cockatiel's common English and American name comes from either the Dutch *kakatielje*, which means "little cockatoo," or the Portuguese *cocatilho*, which means "small parrot." The first birds were exported to Europe in the late 1830s. Color mutations began to develop in the 1950s.

Cockatiels

as **Pets**

Cockatiels make wonderful pets for individuals or families. Their size (12 inches tall and 90 to 110 grams [about 3.5 ounces]) makes them appealing and approachable for children and adults.

Cockatiels offer their owners all the charm and personality of their larger cockatoo cousins without the inherent noise, biting and other problems that come with the larger birds. Cockatiels are long lived (twenty years is not an uncommon life span), they are easy to maintain and affordable to keep.

Although they are not particularly noted for their talking ability, most cockatiels can learn to whistle simple tunes (the theme from *The Andy Griffith Show* seems to be a particular favorite for owners to teach their birds).

Is a Cockatiel the Pet for You?

Before you bring your new cockatiel home, you'll need to consider a few questions. Do you like animals? Do you have time to care for one properly? Can you have pets where you live?

If you've answered "yes" to all these, you're a good candidate for bird ownership.

You'll also need to consider the following: Do you mind a little mess (seed hulls, feathers and discarded food) in your home? Do you mind a little noise (cockatiels sometimes greet the dawn and bid adieu to the sunset with a song) as part of your daily routine? Are you allergic to dust and dander (some people find that cockatiels make them sneeze)? If the answer to these questions is "yes," perhaps you should consider another kind of pet. If the answer is "no," however, a cockatiel may be just the bird for you!

It is recommended that pet owners acquire young hand-fed cockatiels, if possible. The birds are weaned and eating on their own when they are about eight weeks old. Most breeders and pet stores have quite a few young birds available from April to September.

To maintain their lovable personalities, cockatiels need companionship. If you can't devote about a half hour every day to paying attention to your bird, either don't adopt her or make sure she has a cockatiel companion. That half hour could be spent cuddling on the couch while you watch a sitcom, eating breakfast or dinner together or having your bird on a playgym in your bedroom while you get ready in the morning. You can also spend time with your bird while making safe toys for her (such as stringing Cheerios or raw pasta on some bird-safe, vegetable-tanned leather), trick training her or building her a playgym.

Most cockatiels do not talk, but they love to whistle!

The Bottom Line

Some things you'll want to think about before you become a cockatiel owner are:

- the cost of the bird herself
- the cost of her cage and accessories
- the cost of bird food (seeds, formulated diets and fresh foods)
- the cost of toys
- the cost of veterinary care
- the amount of time you can devote to your bird each day
- how busy your life is already
- who will care for the bird if you go on vacation or are called out of town unexpectedly
- how many other pets you already own
- the size of your home

These nestling cockatiels are being hand-fed, or raised by people.

Where to Get Your Cockatiel

Cockatiels can be purchased through several sources, including classified newspaper advertisements, which are usually placed by private parties who want to place pets in new homes; bird shows and marts, which offer breeders and buyers an opportunity to get together and share their love of birds; and pet stores, which may or may not actually sell live animals. Stores that sell livestock are listed as "pet stores" in the phone book, while those that offer food, toys, treats, cages and other pet-care accessories would fall into the category of "pet supply stores."

WHAT'S THAT BAND MEAN?

As you select your pet, you may notice leg bands on the cockatiels you're looking at and may wonder why the birds are wearing them. Bird bands serve several purposes. First, they help identify a particular breeder's stock. They can also help establish an age for your bird, since many of them have the year of hatch as part of the band's code. Finally, some states require that pet birds be banded with closed, traceable bands so that the origin of the bird can be determined in an effort to reduce the number of smuggled birds that are kept as pets in the United States. Although this requirement doesn't apply to cockatiels, it is an indication of things to come in aviculture.

The smooth feathers and full-chested appearance of this cockatiel indicate good health.

Although bands are important for record-keeping purposes, they also have the potential to injure your cockatiel. If you have a particularly skittish bird and she catches her leg band on a frayed cage cover, a perch, a toy or on part of the cage itself, your bird may panic and injure herself severely—even to the point of death—in her efforts to free herself. Also, if your cockatiel injures her leg, the band could further complicate the injury by acting as a tourniquet and cutting off blood supply to the injured leg.

While most cockatiels can wear their leg bands successfully for their entire lives without injuring themselves, you may want to discuss removing your bird's

13

leg band with your avian veterinarian. If you do opt to have the band removed, be sure to keep it in a safe place in case you ever have to prove that your cockatiel was domestically raised, such as if you take the bird out of the country with you should your family move to a foreign country.

HAND-FED OR PARENT-RAISED?

Regardless of where you purchase your cockatiel, try to find a hand-fed bird. Although hand-fed birds cost a bit more than parent-raised ones, hand-fed cockatiels have been raised by people. This process emphasizes the bird's pet qualities and ensures that she will bond with people. You must be willing to spend time playing with and handling your hand-fed cockatiel every day to keep her tame.

Parent-raised chicks may take extra handling and care to become cuddly, easy to handle pets, so they are better candidates for breeding programs. As their name suggests, parent-raised birds have imprinted on their parents and will act like birds when it comes time to raise chicks. Hand-fed pets, however, may pay more attention to their human companions than to other birds, so they may not make ideal candidates for breeding situations.

In the larger parrots, hand-fed birds generally make better pets than their parent-raised counterparts, so you may want to take the extra time and spend a little more money to purchase a hand-fed cockatiel.

SELECTING YOUR COCKATIEL

Once you've located a source for hand-fed cockatiels, it's time to get down to selecting your pet.

MY FIRST COCKATIEL

Stanley eyed me curiously with one bright black eye from inside the small pet carrier. He was a young cockatiel on his way to Texas with a friend of mine. I had agreed to help socialize him to strangers before he made his big trip from the breeder's house to his new home.

I bent down by the carrier and talked to him softly, and he chirped a reply. My friend asked if I wanted to take him out of the carrier, which I did. I carefully opened the lid and Stanley hopped right out of the carrier. I offered Stanley my hand as a perch. Again, he gave it a careful look with one eye, then the other. After deciding it looked like a safe, sturdy place to sit, he climbed onto my finger. Stanley soon made his way up my arm and was nuzzling my neck. My appreciation for curious, affectionate cockatiels had begun.

—Julie Rach

First, observe the birds that are available for sale. If possible, sit down and watch them for awhile. Take note of the birds that seem bolder than the others. Consider those first, because you want a curious, active, robust pet, rather than a shy animal that hides in a corner.

If possible, let your cockatiel choose you. Many pet stores display their cockatiels in colony situations on playgyms, or a breeder may bring out a clutch of babies for you to look at. If one bird waddles right up to you and wants to play, or if one comes over to check you out and just seems to want to come home with you, she's the bird for you!

Ten Steps to Better Bird Care

Some potential bird owners may be put off by the notion that keeping a bird is more difficult than keeping a dog or a cat. While it might seem challenging, bird keeping isn't particularly difficult. I've put together a list of ten simple things that bird owners should do to help keep their pets healthy and safe. Each step will be discussed in more detail in subsequent chapters, but here they are in a brief summary:

Choose a cage with appropriate sized bar spacing and accessories designed for cockatiels.

First, **provide a safe, secure cage in a safe, secure location** in your home. This cage should have appropriate-sized bar spacing and accessories that are designed for cockatiels. It also should be located in a part of your home that you and your family spend time in regularly to help your bird feel part of your daily routine.

Next, **change the cage paper, food and water bowls daily** (be sure to wash the bowls thoroughly with soap and water and rinse them completely), and scrub the cage every week to protect your pet from illness and to make her surroundings more enjoyable for both of you.

Taking your cockatiel to an avian veterinarian for regular checkups is an excellent preventive health measure.

Third, **clip your bird's wings regularly** to ensure her safety. Be particularly alert to new wing feathers that grow in following a molt. Close windows and doors securely before you let your bird out of her cage. You should also keep your bird indoors when she isn't caged and ensure that your pet doesn't chew on anything harmful or become poisoned by toxic fumes from overheated nonstick cookware, cleaning products and other household products.

Fourth, **offer your cockatiel a varied diet** that includes seeds or pellets, small portions of fresh vegetables and fruits, and healthy people food. Provide the freshest food possible, and remove partially eaten or discarded food from the cage before it has a chance to spoil and make your pet sick. Your bird should also have access to clean, fresh drinking water at all times.

Next, **establish a good working relationship with a qualified avian veterinarian** early on in your bird ownership (preferably on your way home from the pet store or breeder). Don't wait for an emergency to locate a veterinarian.

THINGS TO LOOK FOR WHEN CHOOSING A HEALTHY COCKATIEL

bright eyes

a clean cere (the area above the bird's beak that covers her nares or nostrils)

upright posture

a full-chested appearance

actively moving around the cage

clean legs and vent

smooth feathers

good appetite

Sixth, take your cockatiel to the veterinarian for **regular checkups,** as well as when you notice a change in her routine. Illnesses in birds are sometimes difficult to detect before it's too late to save the bird, so preventive care helps head off serious problems before they develop.

Seventh, **maintain a routine for your cockatiel.** Make sure she's fed at about the same time each day, her playtime out of her cage occurs regularly and that her bedtime is well established.

Eighth, **provide an interesting environment for your bird.** Make her feel that she's part of your family. Entertain and challenge your bird's curiosity with a variety of safe toys. Rotate these toys in and out of your bird's cage regularly, and discard any that become soiled, broken, frayed, worn or otherwise unsafe.

Ninth, **leave a radio or television on for your bird when you are away from home.** An extremely quiet environment can be stressful for many birds, and stress can cause illness or other problems for your pet.

Finally, **pay attention to your cockatiel on a consistent basis.** Don't lavish abundant attention on the bird when you first bring her home, then gradually lose interest in her. Birds are sensitive, intelligent creatures that will not understand mixed messages. Set aside a portion of each day to spend with your cockatiel—you'll both enjoy it and your relationship will continue to grow. Besides, wasn't companionship one of the things you were looking for when you picked your cockatiel as a pet?

Simple steps, such as providing a varied diet and a stimulating environment, make for a happy cockatiel.

Now that doesn't seem too difficult, does it? Just devote a little time each day to your pet bird, and soon the two of you will have formed a lifelong bond of trust and mutual enjoyment.

17

Living

with a

Cockatiel

Bringing
Your Cockatiel
Home

Give your cockatiel a chance to gradually get used to your family's routine after you bring him home. Your new pet will need time to adjust to his new environment, so be patient. After you set your cockatiel up in his cage for the first time, spend a few minutes talking quietly to your new pet, and use his name frequently while you're talking. Describe the room he's living in, or tell him about your family.

Adjustment Time

After a couple of days of adjustment, your cockatiel should start to settle into his routine. You will be able to tell when your new pet has adjusted to your home because healthy cockatiels will spend about equal amounts of time during the day eating, playing, sleeping and defecating. By observation, you will soon recognize your pet's normal routine. You may also notice that your bird fluffs or shakes his feathers to greet you, or that he chirps a greeting when you uncover his cage in the morning.

Don't become alarmed the first time you see your cockatiel asleep. Although it seems that your bird has lost his head or a leg, he's fine. Sleeping on one foot with his head tucked under his wing (actually with his head turned about 180 degrees and his beak tucked into the feathers on the back of his neck) is a normal sleeping position for many parrots, although it looks a bit unusual or uncomfortable to bird owners. Be aware, too, that your bird will occasionally perch on one leg while resting the other.

After a few days with your new cockatiel, you will notice that he has a unique personality and routine.

It is very important to have a radio or television on for your cockatiel if you leave him home alone for long periods of time. Although cockatiels have been kept as pets for many years, they may still instinctively hearken back to their wild roots at times. In the grasslands of Australia, silence usually indicates a predator in the area, which can raise a bird's stress level and may make him more susceptible to illness.

A Word about Kids and Cockatiels

If you plan to purchase a cockatiel as a child's pet, please keep in mind that children in the primary grades may need some help caring for their new pet from their parents or from older siblings, while children in the intermediate grades should be ready for the responsibility of bird ownership with limited

21

parental supervision. The bird can also be considered "a family pet" with each family member being responsible for some aspect of the bird's care. Even the youngest family members can help out by selecting healthful foods for the bird on a trip to the market or picking out a safe, colorful toy at the bird store.

Children need to keep the following rules in mind when they're around birds:

- Approach the cage quietly. Birds don't like to be surprised.
- Talk softly to the bird. Don't scream or yell at him.
- Don't shake or hit the cage.
- Don't poke at the bird or his cage with your fingers, sticks, pencils or other items.
- If you're allowed to take the bird out of his cage, handle him gently.
- Don't take the bird outside. In unfamiliar surroundings (such as the outdoors), birds can become confused and fly away from their owners. Most are never recovered.
- Respect the bird's need for quiet time.

I'd like to discourage adults from giving any live pet as a holiday present. Birthdays, Christmas, Hanukkah and other holidays are exciting, but stressful, times for both people and animals.

A pet coming to a new home is under enough stress just by joining his new family; don't add to his stress by bringing him home for a holiday. Instead, give the child pet care accessories for the actual celebration and a gift certificate that will allow the child to select his or her pet (with proper parental permission, of course) after the excitement of the special day has died down somewhat.

Your Cockatiel's Home

Selecting your cockatiel's cage will be one of the most important decisions you will make for your pet, and where that cage will be located in your home is equally important. Don't wait until you bring your bird home to think this through. You'll want your new pet to settle into his surroundings right away, rather than adding to his stress by relocating him several times before selecting the right spot for his cage.

CHOOSING A CAGE

When selecting a cage for your cockatiel, make sure the bird has room to spread his wings without touching the cage sides. His tail should not touch the cage bottom, nor should his crest brush the top. A cage that measures 18×18×24 inches is the minimum size for a single cockatiel, and bigger is always better. If you are planning to keep a pair of birds, the cage should be at least 24×24×40 inches.

Simply put, buy the largest cage you can afford because you don't want your pet to feel cramped. Remember, too, that any parrot is like a little airplane, flying across an area, rather than a little helicopter that hovers up and down. For this reason, long, rectangular cages that offer horizontal space for short flights are preferred to high, tall cages that don't provide much flying room.

Chances are that you'll select a wire cage for your cockatiel. Some cages are sold as part of a cockatiel start-up kit, while others are sold simply as cages. Discuss your options with the salesperson at your local pet supply store. Find out what advantages there are to purchasing a complete kit.

> **AMENITIES FOR YOUR COCKATIEL**
>
> - a cage
> - food and water bowls (at least two sets of each for easier dish changing and cage cleaning)
> - perches of varying diameters and materials
> - a sturdy scrub brush to clean the perches
> - food (a good-quality fresh seed mixture or a formulated diet, such as pellets or crumbles)
> - a powdered vitamin and mineral supplement to sprinkle on your pet's fresh foods
> - a variety of safe, fun toys
> - a cage cover (an old sheet or towel that is free of holes and ravels will serve this purpose nicely)
> - a playgym to allow your cockatiel time out of his cage and a place to exercise

Regardless of whether it's a kit or pre-built, examine any cage you choose carefully before making your final selection. Make sure that the finish is not chipped, bubbled or peeling, because your pet may find the spot and continue removing the finish, which can cause a cage to look old and worn before its time. Also, your pet could become ill if he ingests any of the finish.

Reject any cages that have sharp interior wires or wide bar spacing. (Recommended bar spacing for cockatiels is about 1/2 inch.) Sharp wires could poke your bird, he could become caught between bars that are slightly wider than recommended or he could escape through widely spaced bars. Also be aware that birds can injure themselves on ornate scrollwork that decorates some cages. Finally, make sure the cage you choose has some horizontal bars in it so your cockatiel will be able to climb the cage walls easily for exercise.

Once you've checked the overall cage quality and the bar spacing, look at the cage door. Does it open easily for you, yet remain secure enough to keep your bird in his cage when you close the door? Is it wide enough for you to get your hand in and out of the cage comfortably? Will your bird's food bowl or a bowl of bath water fit through it easily? Does the door open up, down or to the side? Some bird owners prefer that their pets have a play porch on a door that opens drawbridge style, while others are happy with doors that open to the side. Watch out for guillotine-style doors that slide up and over the cage entrance, because some birds have suffered broken legs when the door dropped on them unexpectedly.

Next, look at the cage tray. Does it slide in and out of the cage easily? Remember that you will be changing the paper in this tray at least once a day for the rest of your bird's life (about fifteen years with good care). Is the tray an odd shape or size? Will paper need to be cut into unusual shapes to fit in it, or will paper towels, newspapers or clean sheets of used computer paper fit easily into it? The easier the tray is to remove

Linings made of wood shavings, sand, ground corncobs or walnut shells require diligent cleaning as they tend to hide waste and discarded food.

and reline, the more likely you will be to change the lining of the tray daily. Can the cage tray be replaced if it becomes damaged and unusable? Ask your pet store staff before making your purchase.

Finally, check the floor of the cage you've chosen. Does it have a grille that will keep your bird out of the debris that falls to the bottom of the cage, such as feces, seed hulls, molted feathers and discarded food? To ensure your pet's long-term health, it's best to have a grille between your curious pet and the remains in the cage tray. It's also easier to keep your cockatiel in his cage while you're cleaning the cage tray if there's a grille between the cage and the tray.

WHAT TO PUT IN THE CAGE TRAY

It is recommended that you use clean black-and-white newsprint, paper towels or clean sheets of used computer printer paper. Sand, ground corncobs or walnut shells may be sold by your pet supply store, but are not recommended as cage flooring materials because they tend to hide feces and discarded food quite well. This can cause a bird owner to forget to change the cage tray on the principle that if it doesn't look dirty, it must not be dirty. This line of thinking can set up a thriving, robust colony of bacteria in the bottom of your bird's cage, which can lead to a sick bird if you're not careful. Newsprint and other paper products don't hide the dirt; in fact, they seem to draw attention to it, which leads conscientious bird owners to keep their pets' homes scrupulously clean.

You may see sandpaper or "gravel paper" sold in some pet stores as a cage tray liner. This product is supposed to provide a bird with an opportunity to ingest grit, which is purported to aid indigestion by providing coarse grinding material that helps break up food in the bird's gizzard. However, many avian experts do not believe that a pet bird needs grit, and if a bird stands on rough sandpaper, it could cause foot problems. For your pet's health, please don't use these gravel-coated papers.

COCKATIEL SUPPLIES

You will need the following supplies for your cockatiel:

cage of appropriate size

several different sized perches

safe toys

food and water dishes

cloth for cage cover

high quality seed mix or pelleted food

Cage Location

Now that you've picked the perfect cage for your pet, where will you put it in your home? Your cockatiel will be happiest when he's part of the family, so the living room, family room or dining room may be among the best places for your bird. If your cockatiel is a child's pet, he may do well living in his young owner's room. (Parents should check on the bird regularly, though, to ensure that he's being fed and watered and that his cage is clean.)

Avoid keeping your bird in the bathroom or kitchen, though, because sudden temperature fluctuations or fumes from cleaning products used in those rooms could harm your pet. Another spot to avoid is a busy hall or entryway, because the activity level in these spots may be too much for your pet. Set up the cage so that it is at your eye level if possible, because it will make servicing the cage and visiting with your pet easier for you. It will also reduce the stress on your cockatiel, because birds like to be up high for security. Also, they do not like to have people or things looming over them, so reconsider placing him near items such as ceiling fans, chandeliers or swag lamps. If members of your family are particularly tall, they may want to sit next to the cage or crouch down slightly to talk to the cockatiel.

Regardless of the room you select for your cockatiel, be sure to put the cage in a secure corner (with one solid wall behind the cage to ensure your cockatiel's sense of security); near a window is recommended. Please don't put the cage in direct sun, though, because cockatiels can quickly overheat.

A food crock, or shallow dish, allows your cockatiel to snack throughout the day.

CAGE ACCESSORIES

Along with the perfect-sized cage in the ideal location in your home, your pet will need a few cage accessories. These include food and water dishes, perches, toys and a cage cover.

FOOD DISHES

Cockatiels seem to enjoy food crocks, which are open ceramic bowls that allow them to hop up on the edge of the bowl and pick and choose what they will during the day. Be sure to purchase shallow dishes that are less than one inch deep to ensure that your bird has easy access to his food at all times. When purchasing dishes for your cockatiel, be sure to pick up several sets so that mealtime cleanups are quick and easy.

PERCHES

When choosing perches for your pet's cage, try to buy two different diameters of materials so your bird's feet won't get tired of standing on the same-sized perch made of the same material day after day. Think of how tired your feet would feel if you stood on a piece of wood in your bare feet all day, then imagine how it would feel to stand on that piece of wood barefoot every day for ten or fifteen years. Sounds pretty uncomfortable, doesn't it? That's basically what your bird has to look forward to if you don't vary his perching choices.

Vary the sizes, types and levels of perches to relieve foot muscle fatigue as well as to provide a sleeping roost for your cockatiel.

The recommended diameter for cockatiel perches is 5/8 inch, so try to buy one perch that's this size and one that is slightly larger (3/4 inch, for example) to give your pet a chance to stretch his foot muscles. Birds spend almost all of their lives standing, so keeping their feet healthy is important. Also, avian foot problems are much easier to prevent than they are to treat.

You'll probably notice a lot of different kinds of perches when you visit your pet store. Along with the traditional wooden dowels, bird owners can now purchase perches made from manzanita branches, PVC tubes, rope perches and terra-cotta or concrete grooming perches.

Manzanita offers birds varied diameters on the same perch, along with chewing possibilities, while PVC is almost indestructible. (Make sure any PVC perches you offer your bird have been scuffed slightly with sandpaper to improve traction on the perch.) Rope perches also offer varied diameter and a softer perching surface than wood or plastic, and terra-cotta and concrete provide slightly abrasive surfaces that birds can use to groom their beaks without severely damaging the skin on their feet in the process. Some bird owners have reported that their pets have suffered foot abrasions with these perches, however; watch your pet carefully for signs of sore feet (an inability to perch or climb, favoring a foot or raw, sore skin on the feet) if you choose to use these perches in your pet's cage. If your bird shows signs of lameness, remove the abrasive perches immediately and arrange for your avian veterinarian to examine your bird.

To further help your bird avoid foot problems, do not use sandpaper covers on his perches. These sleeves, touted as nail-trimming devices, really do little to trim a parrot's nails because birds don't usually drag their nails along their perches. What the sandpaper perch covers are good at doing, though, is abrading the surface of your cockatiel's feet, which can leave them vulnerable to infections and can make moving about the cage painful for your pet.

When placing perches in your bird's cage, try to vary the heights slightly so your bird has different "levels" in his cage. Don't place any perches over food or water dishes, because birds can and will contaminate food or water by defecating in it. Finally, place one perch higher than the rest for a nighttime sleeping roost. Cockatiels and other parrots like to sleep on the highest point they can find to perch, so please provide this security to your pet.

CHOOSING THE RIGHT TOYS

When selecting toys for your pet, keep a few safety tips in mind. First, is the toy the right size for your bird? Large toys can be intimidating to small birds, which makes the birds less likely to play with them. On the other end of the spectrum, larger parrots can easily destroy toys designed for smaller birds, and they can sometimes injure themselves severely in the process.

Cockatiels enjoy the following types of toys: chewable wooden items, ranging from clothes pegs (not clothespins, which have potentially dangerous springs that can snap on a bird's wing or leg) to spools; wooden ladders, sturdy ropes or cords to climb on; bells to ring; knotted rope or leather toys to preen and chew on; and mirrors to admire themselves in. Be warned, though, that if you give a single cockatiel a mirror toy, he may bond to the reflection he sees and consider the bird in the mirror a more interesting companion than you!

Sturdy wooden toys strung on closed-link chains and rope toys are recommended for your cockatiel.

As an alternative to store-bought toys, you can entertain your cockatiel with some everyday items you have around the house. Give your bird an empty paper towel roll or toilet paper tube (from unscented paper only, please) to chew. Let him shred subscription cards from your favorite magazines or chew up some clean computer paper. Give him a Ping-Pong ball to chase. String some Cheerios on a piece of vegetable-tanned leather, or offer your bird a dish of raw pasta pieces to destroy.

When you're introducing new toys to your cockatiel for the first time, you might want to leave the toy next to the cage for a few days before actually putting it in the cage. Some birds accept new items in their cages almost immediately, but others need a few days to size up a new toy, dish or perch before sharing cage space with it.

Be sure to evaluate if the toy is safe. Good choices include sturdy wooden toys (either undyed or painted with bird-safe vegetable dye or food coloring) strung on closed-link chains or vegetable-tanned leather thongs, and rope toys. If you purchase rope toys for your cockatiel, make sure his nails are trimmed regularly to prevent them from snagging in the rope, and discard the toy when it becomes frayed to prevent accidents from happening.

> ### HOMEMADE TOYS
>
> Entertaining and safe toys can be made at home. Give your bird an empty paper towel roll or toilet paper tube (from unscented paper only, please), string some Cheerios on a piece of vegetable-tanned leather or offer your bird a dish of raw pasta pieces to destroy.

Unsafe items to watch out for are brittle plastic toys that can be shattered easily by a cockatiel's beak, lead-weighted toys that can be cracked open to expose the dangerous lead to curious birds, loose-link chains that can catch toenails or beaks, ring toys that are too small to climb through safely or jingle-type bells that can trap toes, tongues or beaks.

THE CAGE COVER

One important, but sometimes overlooked, accessory is the cage cover. Be sure that you have something to cover your cockatiel's cage with when it's time to put your pet to sleep each night. The act of covering the cage seems to calm many pet birds and convince them that it's really time to go to bed despite the sounds of an active family evening in the background.

You can purchase a cage cover, or you can use an old sheet, blanket or towel that is clean and free of holes. Be aware that some birds like to chew on their cage covers through the cage bars. If your bird does this, replace the cover when it becomes too tattered to do its job effectively. Replacing a well-chewed cover will also help keep your bird from becoming entangled in the cover or caught in a ragged clump of threads. Some birds have injured themselves quite severely by being caught in a chewed cage cover, so help keep your pet safe from this hazard.

Cockatiels may also benefit from a night-light being left on for them at bedtime. Some cockatiels are prone to night frights, in which they thrash around the cage and can injure themselves quite seriously. Having a low-wattage light on helps these birds find their way around the cage at night, which may make them less prone to being startled.

Ladders, swings, perches and toys stimulate your cockatiel and also provide opportunity for exercise.

THE PLAYGYM

Although your cockatiel will spend quite a bit of time in his cage, he will also need time out of his cage to exercise and to enjoy a change of scenery. A playgym can help keep your pet physically and mentally active.

If you visit a large pet store or bird specialty store, or if you look through the pages of any pet bird hobbyist magazine, you will see a variety of playgyms on display. You can choose a complicated gym with a series of ladders, swings, perches and toys, or you can purchase a simple T-stand that has a place for food and water bowls and a screw or two from which you can hang toys. If you're really handy with tools, you can even construct a gym to your cockatiel's specifications.

As with the cage, location of your cockatiel's playgym will be a consideration. You will want to place the gym in a secure location in your home that is safe from other curious pets, ceiling fans, open windows and other household hazards. You will also want the gym to be in a spot frequented by your family, so your bird will have company while he plays and supervision so he doesn't get into unsafe situations.

chapter 4

Grooming

Your **Cockatiel**

Your cockatiel has several grooming needs. First, she must be able to bathe regularly, and she will need to have her nails and flight feathers trimmed periodically to ensure her safety.

Although some people would say that a cockatiel's beak also needs trimming, I would argue that a healthy bird that has enough chew toys does a remarkable job of keeping its beak trimmed. If your bird's beak becomes overgrown, though, please consult your avian veterinarian. A parrot's beak contains a surprising number of blood vessels, so beak trimming is best left to the experts. Also, a suddenly overgrown beak may indicate that your bird is suffering from liver damage, a virus or scaly mites, all of which require veterinary care.

34

Bathing

You can bathe your bird in a variety of ways. You can mist her lightly with a clean spray bottle filled with warm water only, you can allow her to bathe in the kitchen or bathroom sink under a slow stream of water or you can take her into the shower with you. Bathing is important to birds to help them keep their feathers clean and healthy, so don't deny your pet the chance to bathe!

Unless your cockatiel has gotten herself into oil, paint, wax or some other substance that elbow grease alone won't remove and that could harm her feathers, she will not require soap as part of her bath. Under routine conditions, soaps and detergents can damage a bird's feathers by removing beneficial oils, so hold the shampoo during your cockatiel's normal bath!

Let your bird bathe early in the day so her feathers can dry completely before bedtime. In cooler weather, you may want help the process along by drying your pet off with a blow-dryer to prevent her from becoming chilled after her bath. To do this, set the blow-dryer on low and keep it moving so that your bird doesn't become overheated. Your bird may soon learn (as mine has) that drying off is the most enjoyable part of her bath!

While we're discussing grooming and feather care, please don't purchase mite protectors that hang on a bird's cage or conditioning products that are applied directly to a bird's feathers. Well-cared-for cockatiels don't have mites and shouldn't be in danger of contracting them. (If your pet does have mites, veterinary care is the most effective treatment method.) Also, the fumes from some of these products are quite strong and can be harmful to your pet's health. Conditioners, anti-picking products and other substances that are applied to your bird's feathers will serve one purpose: to get your bird to preen herself so thoroughly that she could remove all her feathers in a particular area. If you want to encourage your bird to preen regularly and help condition her feathers, simply mist the bird regularly with clean, warm water or hold her under a gentle stream from a kitchen or bathroom faucet. Your bird will take care of the rest.

Nail Care

Cockatiels and other parrots need their nails clipped occasionally to prevent the nails from catching on toys or perches and injuring the bird. Lutino cockatiels have light-colored nails, which make it easier for owners to see where the nail stops and the blood and nerve supply (or quick) begins. In lutinos, the quick is generally seen as a pink color inside the nail. Owners of other color mutations will have to pare down their birds' nails carefully to ensure that they do not cut the quick.

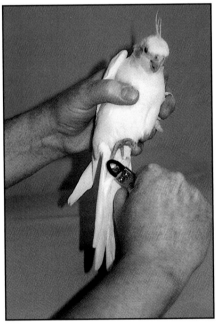

Only tiny portions of the nail need to be removed to keep your cockatiel's claws trimmed.

You will need to remove only tiny portions of the nail to keep your cockatiel's claws trimmed. Generally, a good guideline to follow is to only remove the hook on each nail, and to do this in the smallest increments possible. Stop well before you reach the quick. If you do happen to cut the nail short enough to make it bleed, apply cornstarch or flour, followed by direct pressure, to stop the bleeding.

Wing Trimming

Cockatiels are among the fastest flying pet birds. Their sleek, slender bodies give them an advantage over larger birds, such as Amazons and African greys. Since cockatiels are so aerodynamic, owners must pay close attention to the condition of the bird's wing feathers and trim them regularly to keep the bird safe. The goal of a proper wing trim is to prevent your pet from flying away or into a window, mirror or wall while she's out of her cage. An added benefit of trimming your pet's wings is that her inability to fly well will make her more dependent on you for transportation, which should make her more handleable. However, the bird still needs enough wing feathers so that if she is startled and takes flight from her cage top or playgym she can glide safely to the ground.

Because this is a delicate balance, you may want to enlist the help of your avian veterinarian, at least the first time. Wing trimming is a task that must be performed carefully to avoid injuring your pet, so take your time if you're doing it yourself. Please *do not* just take up the largest pair of kitchen shears you own and start snipping away, as this can cause severe injury to the bird's wingtips.

WHAT YOU'LL NEED

The first step in wing feather trimming is to assemble your supplies and find a quiet, well-lit place to groom your pet before you catch her. Your grooming tools will include

- a well-worn washcloth or small towel to wrap your bird in

- small, sharp scissors to do the actual trimming

- needle-nosed pliers (to pull any blood feathers you may cut accidentally)

- flour or cornstarch to act as styptic powder in case a blood feather is cut

I encourage you to groom your pet in a quiet, well-lit place because grooming excites some birds and causes them to become wiggly. Having good light to work under will make your job easier, and having a quiet work area may calm your pet and make her more handleable.

37

GETTING STARTED

Once you've assembled your supplies, drape the towel over your hand and catch your bird with your toweled hand. Hold your bird by the back of her head and neck, and wrap her in the towel. Support your bird's head securely with your thumb and index finger. (Having the bird's head covered by the towel will calm her and will give her something to chew on while you clip her wings.)

Lay the bird gently on her back, being careful not to constrict or compress her chest (remember, birds have no diaphragms to help them breathe) and spread her wing out carefully to look for blood feathers hat are still growing in. These can be identified by their waxy, tight look and their dark centers or quills, which are caused by the blood supply to the new feather.

CAREFUL TRIMMING

If your bird has a number of blood feathers, you may want to put off trimming her wings for a few days, because fully grown feathers cushion those just coming in from hard knocks. If your bird has only one or two blood feathers, you can trim the rest accordingly.

To trim your bird's feathers, separate each one away from the other flight feathers and cut it individually (remember, the goal is to have a well-trimmed bird that's still able to glide a bit if it needs to). Use the primary coverts (the set of feathers above the primary flight feathers on your bird's wing) as a safe guideline to monitor how short you can trim.

Cut the first six to eight flight feathers starting from the tip of the wing, and be sure to trim an equal number of feathers from each wing. Although some people think that a bird needs only one trimmed wing, this is incorrect and could actually cause harm to a bird that tries to fly with one trimmed and one untrimmed wing.

About Blood Feathers

If you do happen to cut a blood feather, remain calm. You must remove it and stop the bleeding, and panicking will do neither you nor your bird much good.

To remove a blood feather, take a pair of needle-nosed pliers and grasp the broken feather's shaft as close to the skin of your bird's wing as you can. With one steady motion, pull the feather out completely. After you've removed the feather, put a pinch of flour or cornstarch on the feather follicle (the spot you pulled the feather out of) and apply direct pressure for a few minutes until the bleeding stops. If the bleeding doesn't stop after a few minutes of direct pressure, or if you can't remove the feather shaft, contact your avian veterinarian for further instructions.

Although it may seem like you're hurting your cockatiel by removing the broken blood feather, consider this: A broken blood feather is like an open faucet. If the feather stays in, the faucet remains open and lets the blood out. Once removed, the bird's skin generally closes up behind the feather shaft and shuts off the faucet.

Now that you've successfully trimmed your bird's wing feathers, congratulate yourself. You've just taken a great step toward keeping your bird safe. But don't rest on your laurels just yet; you must remember to check your bird's wing feathers and retrim them periodically (about four times a year as a minimum).

How Often

Although it may seem like your cockatiel's tail feathers need regular trimming, they don't under normal circumstances. Some cockatiels may thrash their tail feathers in the course of their normal activities, and you may feel better about your bird's appearance if you trim the scruffy-looking feathers. However, if your bird's tail feathers are often damaged or ratty-looking, your cockatiel's cage may be too small for her to move about easily and comfortably. Remember that your pet's cage should be spacious enough for her to move about easily, extend her wings fully and not have her crest touch the cage ceiling or the tip of her tail feathers touch the floor of the cage. If your bird's cage fails these simple tests, purchase a larger cage for your pet and use the smaller cage as a travel cage or as a temporary home when you're cleaning the main cage.

Be particularly alert after a molt, because your bird will have a whole new crop of flight feathers that need attention. You'll be able to tell when your bird is due for a trim when she starts becoming bolder in her flying attempts. Right after a wing trim, a cockatiel generally tries to fly and finds she's unsuccessful at the attempt. She will keep trying, though, and may surprise you one day with a fairly good glide across her cage or off her playgym. If this happens, get the scissors and trim those wings immediately. If you don't, the section that follows on finding lost birds may have more meaning that you can imagine.

Feeding

Your

Cockatiel

Although they live in arid climates, wild cockatiels spend a great deal of their time foraging for ripening grass seeds, which are high in carbohydrates and lower in proteins and fats. This need for sprouted fresh foods makes a simple seed-and-water diet unsuitable for pet birds. Poor diet also causes a number of health problems (respiratory infections, poor feather condition, flaky skin, reproductive problems, to name a few) and is one of the main reasons some cockatiels live fairly short lives.

Nutrition Requirements

According to avian veterinarian Gary Gallerstein, birds require about a dozen vitamins—A, D, E, K, B1, B2, niacin, B6, B12, pantothenic acid, biotin, folic acid and choline—to stay healthy, but they can only partially manufacture D3 and niacin. A balanced diet can help provide the rest.

Offer your cockatiel a variety of vitamin-enriched seeds and nuts along with fresh fruits and vegetables.

Along with the vitamins listed above, pet birds need trace amounts of some minerals to maintain good health. These minerals are calcium, phosphorus, sodium, chlorine, potassium, magnesium, iron, zinc, copper, sulphur, iodine and manganese. These can be provided with a well-balanced diet and a supplemental mineral block or cuttlebone.

Ideally, your cockatiel's diet should contain about equal parts of seed, grain and legumes and dark green or dark orange vegetables and fruits. You can supplement these with small amounts of well-cooked meat or eggs, or dairy products. Let's look at each part of this diet in a little more detail.

SEEDS

First, the seeds, grains and legumes portion of your bird's diet can include clean, fresh seed from your local pet supply store. Try to buy your birdseed from a store where stock turns over quickly. The dusty box on the bottom shelf of a store with little traffic isn't as nutritious for your pet as a bulk purchase of seeds from a freshly filled bin in a busy shop. When you bring the seeds home, refrigerate them to keep them from becoming "buggy."

To ensure your bird is receiving the proper nutrients from its diet, you need to know if the seed you're serving is fresh. One way to do this is to try sprouting some of the seeds. (Sprouted seeds can also tempt a finicky eater to broaden his diet.)

To sprout seeds, you will need to soak them overnight in lukewarm water. Drain the water off and let the seeds sit in a closed cupboard or other out-of-the-way place for twenty-four hours. Rinse the sprouted seeds thoroughly before offering them to your bird. If the seeds don't sprout, they aren't fresh, and you'll need to find another source for your bird's food.

> ### VITAL VITAMINS & MINERALS
>
> The foundation for a healthy cockatiel starts with a balanced diet supplemented by vitamins (A, D, E, K, B1, B2, niacin, B6, B12, pantothenic acid, biotin, folic acid and choline) as well as minerals (calcium, phosphorus, sodium, chlorine, potassium, magnesium, iron, zinc, copper, sulphur, iodine and manganese). A mineral block or cuttlebone will supplement a well-rounded diet.

The seed mixture you feed your cockatiel should be fresh and kept refrigerated until served.

Be sure, too, that your pet has an adequate supply of seeds in its dish at all times. Some cockatiels are such neat eaters that they drop the empty seed hulls back into their dishes. This seemingly full dish can lead to a very hungry cockatiel if an owner isn't observant enough to check the dish carefully. Rather than just looking in the dish while it's in the cage, I suggest that you take the dish out and inspect it over the trash can so you can empty the seed hulls and refill the dish easily.

MILLET

One foodstuff that is very popular with cockatiels is millet, especially millet sprays. These golden sprays are part treat and part toy. Offer your cockatiel this treat sparingly, however, because it is high in fat! Other items in the bread group that you can offer your pet include unsweetened breakfast cereals, whole-wheat bread, cooked beans, cooked rice and pasta.

Fresh fruits and vegetables supply vitamin A, which prevents infection and promotes respiratory health.

FRUITS AND VEGETABLES

Dark green or dark orange vegetables and fruits contain vitamin A, which is an important part of a bird's diet and which is missing from the seeds, grains and legumes group. This vitamin helps fight off infection and keeps a bird's eyes, mouth and respiratory system healthy. Some vitamin A-rich foods are carrots, yams, sweet potatoes, broccoli, dried red peppers, dandelion greens and spinach.

You may be wondering whether or not to offer frozen or canned vegetables and fruits to your bird. Some birds will eat frozen vegetables and fruits, while others turn their beaks up at the somewhat mushy texture of these foodstuffs. The high sodium content in some canned foods may make them unhealthy for your cockatiel. Frozen and canned foods will serve your bird's needs in an emergency, but I would offer only fresh foods on a regular basis.

OTHER FRESH FOODS

Along with small portions of the well-cooked meat I mentioned earlier, you can also offer your bird bits of tofu, water-packed tuna, fully scrambled eggs, cottage cheese, unsweetened yogurt or low-fat cheese. Don't overdo the dairy products, though, because a bird's digestive system lacks the enzyme lactase, which means he is unable to fully process dairy foods.

Introduce young cockatiels to healthy people food early so that they learn to appreciate a varied diet. Some adult birds cling tenaciously to seed-only diets, which aren't as healthy for them in the long term. Offer adult birds fresh foods, too, in the hope that they may try something new.

Whatever healthy fresh foods you offer your pet, be sure to remove food from the cage promptly to prevent spoilage and to help keep your bird healthy. Ideally, you should change the food in your bird's cage every two to four hours (about every thirty minutes in warm weather), so a cockatiel should be all right with a tray of food to pick through in the morning, another to select from during

> ### SPROUTING
>
> Serving sprouts is a simple and nutritious way to expand your cockatiel's diet. Sprouted seeds are packed with vitamins and are a tasty addition to the diet. All you need is a sprouting jar, some mesh cloth and a variety of seeds such as sunflower, mung or radish. A health food store should carry this equipment as well as instructions for sprouting seeds.
>
> The first step in the technique is to wash and soak the seeds. The seeds should then be kept in a warm location to encourage sprouting. It is important that all of the material used is washed well to avoid spoiling. It takes about two to three days for the seed to sprout. Once they have sprouted, offer them to your cockatiel for a nutritious treat.

the afternoon and a third fresh salad to nibble on for dinner.

SUPPLEMENTS

You may also be concerned if your bird is receiving adequate amounts of vitamins and minerals in his diet. If your cockatiel's diet is mostly seeds and fresh foods, you may want to sprinkle a good-quality vitamin-and-mineral powder onto the fresh foods, where it has the best chance of sticking to the food and being eaten. Vitamin-enriched seed diets may provide some supplementation, but some of them add the vitamins and minerals to the seed hull, which your pet will discard while it's eating. Avoid adding vitamin and mineral supplements to your bird's water dish, because they can act as a growth medium for bacteria. They may also cause the water to taste different to your bird, which may discourage him from drinking.

Food and water cups should be washed frequently, especially if your cockatiel likes to sit in them.

WATER

Along with providing fresh foodstuffs at least twice a day, you will need to provide your cockatiel with fresh, clean water twice a day to maintain its good health. One technique is to give fresh water in the morning with vegetables and fruit and to replace the water from the morning that evening when you remove the perishable foods and replace them with seeds or pellets.

The water cups tend to build up a dirty film, so take care to cleanse and rinse them thoroughly. It is also recommended to change the water cup two to three times a day if you are adding vitamins to the water.

Offer your cock-atiel a variety of treats in his cage to keep him interested in his food.

Foods to Avoid

Now that we've looked at foods that are good for your bird, let's look briefly at those that aren't healthy for your pet. Among those foods considered harmful to pet birds are alcohol, rhubarb, avocado (the skin and the area around the pit can be toxic), as well as highly salted, sweetened or fatty foods. You should especially avoid chocolate because it contains a chemical, theobromine, which birds cannot digest as completely as people can. Chocolate can kill your cockatiel, so resist the temptation to share this snack with your pet. You will also want to avoid giving your bird seeds or pits from apples, apricots, cherries, peaches, pears and plums, because they can be harmful to your pet's health.

Let common sense be your guide in choosing which foods can be offered to your bird: If it's healthy for you, it's probably okay to share. However, remember to reduce the size of the portion you offer to your bird—a smaller cockatiel-sized portion will be more appealing to your pet than a larger, human-sized portion.

While sharing healthy people food with your bird is completely acceptable, sharing something that you've already taken a bite of is not. Human saliva has bacteria that are potentially toxic to birds, so please don't share partially eaten food with your pet. For your bird's health and your peace of mind, get him his own portion or plate.

By the same token, please don't kiss your cockatiel on the beak (kiss him on top of his little head instead) or allow your bird to put his head into your mouth, nibble on your lips or preen your teeth. Although you may see birds doing this on television or in magazine pictures, it's really unsafe for your bird's health and well-being.

INGREDIENTS FOR A HEALTHFUL COCKATIEL DIET

Seed Mix

Pellets

Fresh Vegetables

Fruits in smaller amounts

Vitamin supplements

Occasional treats

Along with providing nutrition for your cockatiel, food can serve as a mental diversion. Like their larger cousins the cockatoos, a cockatiel's nimble brain needs challenges throughout the day to keep him from becoming bored.

The Pelleted Diet Option

Cockatiels have played an important role in the creation of pelleted, or formulated, diets for all pet birds. In the early 1980s, researchers at the University of California, Davis, began conducting nutritional research on cockatiels to determine what the best diet for pet birds would be. In order to make fair comparisons of the different nutrients, the researchers created formulated diets for the test flock. Avian nutritionists have used the data gleaned from this test flock in creating many of the pelleted diets that are available today.

Pelleted diets are created by mixing as many as forty different nutrients into a mash and then forcing (or extruding) the hot mixture through a machine to form various shapes. Some pelleted diets have colors and flavors added, while others are fairly plain. These formulated diets provide more balanced nutrition in an easy-to-serve form that reduces the amount of wasted food and eliminates the chance for a bird to pick through a smorgasbord of healthy foods to find its favorites and reject the foods he isn't particularly fond of. Some cockatiels accept pelleted diets quickly, while others require some persuading.

STARTING A PELLETED DIET

To convert your pet to a pelleted diet, offer pellets alongside of or mixed in with his current diet. Once you see that your bird is eating the pellets, begin to gradually increase the amount of pellets you offer at mealtime while decreasing the amount of other food you serve. Within a couple of weeks, your bird should be eating his pellets with gusto!

A well balanced diet will help keep your cockatiel free of respiratory infections, poor feather condition, flaky skin and reproductive problems.

If your cockatiel seems a bit finicky about trying pellets, another bird in the house may show your cockatiel how yummy pellets can be, or you may have to act as if you are enjoying the pellets as a snack in front of your pet. Really play up your apparent enjoyment of this new food because it will pique your bird's curiosity and make the pellets exceedingly interesting to your pet.

Whatever you do, don't starve your bird into trying a new food. Offer new foods along with familiar favorites. This will ensure that your bird is eating and will also encourage it to try new foods. Don't be discouraged if your cockatiel doesn't dive right in to a new food. Be patient, keep offering new foods to your bird, and praise him enthusiastically when he samples something new!

chapter 6

Your Cockatiel's
Physical
Health

In general, cockatiels have a hardy resistance to disease and are very healthy birds. They have a strong survival instinct, and even when ill, cockatiels will continue to "act" normally for long periods of time. Since birds can't describe how they are feeling, it is very important that owners understand the basics of their pet's physiology as well as the signs of illness. Cockatiels, like all other pets, are subject to disease and injury. With preventive measures, early detection and good care, the odds for successful recovery are great.

Avian Anatomy

Your pet cockatiel's body is essentially very similar to that of a mammal. Both have skin, skeletons, respiratory, cardiovascular, digestive, excretory and nervous systems, and sensory organs, although the various systems function in slightly different ways.

INTEGUMENT (SKIN)

Your bird's skin is difficult to see since your pet has so many feathers. If you part the feathers carefully, though, you can see thin, seemingly transparent skin and the muscles beneath it. Modified skin cells help make up your bird's beak, cere, claws and the scales on her feet and legs.

Birds cannot perspire as mammals do because birds have no sweat glands, so they must have a way to cool themselves off. On a warm day, you may notice your bird sitting with her wings held away from her body, rolling her tongue and holding her mouth open. This is how a bird cools itself off. Watch your bird carefully on warm days because she can overheat quickly, and he may suffer from heatstroke, which requires veterinary care. If you live in a warm climate, ask your avian veterinarian how you can protect your bird from this serious problem.

Birds have no sweat glands— they cool themselves by panting and lifting their wings away from their body.

FEATHERS

Birds are the only animals that have feathers, which serve several purposes. Feathers help birds fly, they keep birds warm, they attract the attention of potential mates and they help scare away predators.

Did you know that your cockatiel has between 5,000 and 6,000 feathers on its body? These feathers grow from follicles that are arranged in rows that are known as pterylae. The unfeathered patches of bare skin on your bird's body are called apteria.

A feather is a remarkably designed creation. The base of the feather shaft, which fits into the bird's skin, is called the quill. It is light and hollow, but remarkably tough. The upper part of the feather shaft is called the rachis. From the rachis branch the barbs and barbules (smaller barbs) that make up most of the feather. The barbs and barbules have small hooks on them that enable the different parts of the feather to interlock like Velcro and form the feather's vane or web.

Birds have several different types of feathers on their bodies. *Contour feathers* are the colorful outer feathers on a bird's body and wings. Many birds have an undercoating of *down feathers* that helps keep them warm. *Semiplume feathers* are found on a bird's beak, nares (nostrils) and eyelids.

A bird's *flight feathers* can be classified into one of two types. Primary flight feathers are the large wing feathers that push a bird forward during flight. They are also the ones that need clipping, which we discussed earlier. Secondary flight feathers are found on the inner wing, and they help support the bird in flight. Primary and secondary wing feathers can operate independently of each other. The bird's tail feathers also assist in flight by acting as a brake and a rudder to make steering easier.

Feathers insulate your cockatiel and help to maintain body temperature.

To keep their feathers in good condition, healthy birds spend a great deal of time fluffing and preening their feathers. You may see your cockatiel seeming to pick at the base of her tail on the top side. This is a normal behavior in which the bird removes oil from the preen gland and spreads it on her feathers. The oil

helps prevent skin infections and waterproofs the
feathers.

Sometimes pet birds will develop white lines or small
holes on the large feathers of their wings and tails.
These lines or holes are referred to as "stress bars" or
"stress lines" and result from the bird being under stress
as the feathers were developing. If you notice stress
bars on your bird's feathers, discuss them with your
avian veterinarian. Be prepared to describe anything
new in your pet's routine to the veterinarian, be-cause
parrots are creatures of habit that sometimes react to
changes in their surroundings, diet or daily activities.

MUSCULOSKELETAL SYSTEM

Next, let's look at your bird's skeleton. Did you know
that some bird bones are hollow? These are lighter,
making flying easier, but also meaning that these bones
are more susceptible to breakage. For this reason, you
must always handle your bird carefully! Another adap-
tation for flight is that the bones of a bird's wing
(which correspond to our arm and
hand bones) are fused for greater
strength.

*Cockatiels can
turn their heads
to a greater degree
than other mam-
mals because they
have additional
neck vertebrae.*

Birds also have air sacs in some
of their bones (these are called
pneumatic bones) and in certain
body cavities that help lighten
the bird's body and also cool her
more efficiently.

Parrots have ten neck vertebrae to
a human's seven. This makes a parrot's neck more mobile than a person's (a parrot can turn its head
almost 180 degrees). This gives the
parrot an advantage in spotting
food or predators in the wild.

During breeding season, a female
bird's bones become denser to
enable her to store calcium needed to create eggshells.
A female's skeleton can weigh up to 20 percent more

during breeding season than she does the rest of the year because of this calcium storage.

RESPIRATORY SYSTEM

Your bird's respiratory system is a highly efficient system that works in a markedly different way from yours. Here's how your bird breathes: Air enters the system through your bird's nares, passes through her sinuses and into her throat. As it does, the air is filtered through the choana, which is a slit that can be easily seen in the roof of many birds' mouths. The choana also helps to clean and warm the air before it goes further into the respiratory system.

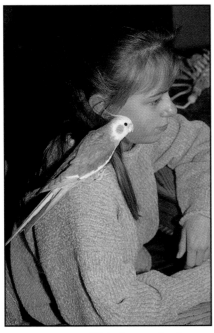

After the air passes the choana, it flows through the larynx and trachea, past the syrinx or "voice box." Your bird doesn't have vocal cords like you do; rather, vibrations of the syrinx membrane are what allow birds to make sounds.

So far it sounds similar to the way we breathe, doesn't it? Well, here's where the differences begin. As the air continues its journey past the syrinx and into the bronchi, your bird's lungs don't expand and contract to bring the air in.

Cockatiels take two breaths for every one breath taken by a human.

This is partly due to the fact that birds don't have diaphragms like people do. Instead, the bird's body wall expands and contracts, much like a fireplace bellows. This action brings air into the air sacs mentioned earlier as part of the skeleton. This bellows action also moves air in and out of the lungs.

Although a bird's respiratory system is extremely efficient at exchanging gases in the system, two complete breaths are required to do the same work that a single breath does in people and other mammals. This is why you may notice that your bird seems to be breathing quite quickly.

CARDIOVASCULAR SYSTEM

Along with the respiratory system, your bird's cardio-vascular system keeps oxygen and other nutrients moving throughout your pet's body, although the circulatory path in your cockatiel differs from yours. In your cockatiel, blood flowing from the legs, reproductive system and lower intestines passes through the kidneys on its way back to the general circulatory system.

The underside of the beak has small ridges that help your cockatiel crack seeds.

DIGESTIVE SYSTEM

Your bird's body needs fuel for energy. Birds' bodies are fueled by food, which is where your bird's digestive system comes in. The digestive system provides the fuel that maintains your bird's body temperature. A bird's body temperature is higher than a human's. The first time I bird-sat for friends, I worried about their cockatoo's seemingly hot feet. After another bird owner told me that birds have higher temperatures than people, I stopped worrying about the bird's warm feet.

Your cockatiel's digestive system begins with its beak. The size and shape of a bird's beak depend on its food-gathering needs. Compare the sharp, pointed beak of an eagle or the elongated bill of a humming-bird with the small, hooked beak of your cockatiel.

Because cockatiels eat primarily seeds and other plant materials, their beaks have developed into efficient little seed crackers. Notice the underside of your bird's upper beak if you can. It has tiny ridges in it that help your cockatiel hold and crack seeds more easily.

A parrot's mouth works differently than a mammal's. Parrots don't have saliva to break down and move their food like we do. After the food leaves your bird's mouth, it travels down the esophagus, where it is moistened. The food then travels to the crop, where it is moistened further and emptied in small increments into the bird's stomach.

After the food leaves the crop, it travels through the proventriculus, where digestive juices are added, then to the gizzard, where the food is broken down into even smaller pieces. The food next travels to the small intestine, where nutrients are absorbed into the bloodstream. Anything that's left over travels through the large intestine to the cloaca, which is the common chamber that collects wastes before they leave the bird's body through the vent. The whole process from mouth to vent usually takes only a few hours, which is why you may notice that your bird leaves frequent, small droppings in its cage.

Along with the solid waste created by the digestive system, your cockatiel's kidneys create urine, which is transported through ureters to the cloaca for excretion. Unlike a mammal, a bird does not have a bladder or a urethra.

NERVOUS SYSTEM

Your cockatiel's nervous system is very similar to your own. Both are made up of the brain, the spinal cord and countless nerves throughout the body that transmit messages to and from the brain.

THE SENSES

Taste

Compared to other mammals, the sense of taste is poorly developed in cockatiels. Birds *can* taste, but in limits due to the small number and location of taste buds (on the roof of the mouth rather than the tongue).

Vision

Cockatiels have a well-developed sense of sight. Birds see detail and they can discern colors. Be aware of this when selecting cage accessories for your pet because some birds react to changes in the color of their food dishes. Some seem excited by a different color bowl, while others act fearful of the new item.

Because their eyes are located on the sides of their heads, most pet birds rely on monocular vision, which means that they use each eye independent of the other. If a bird wants to study an object, you will see her tilt her head to one side and examine the object with just one eye. Birds aren't really able to move their eyes around very much, but they compensate for this by having highly mobile necks that allow them to turn their heads about 180 degrees.

Like cats and dogs, birds have third eyelids called nictitating membranes that you will sometimes see flick briefly across your cockatiel's eye. The purpose of this membrane is to keep the eyeball moist and clean. If you see your cockatiel's nictitating membrane for more than a brief second, contact your avian veterinarian for an evaluation. You have probably noticed that your bird lacks eyelashes. In their place are small feathers called semiplumes that help keep dirt and dust out of the bird's eyeball.

Hearing

You may be wondering where your bird's ears are. Look carefully under the feathers behind and below each eye to find them. The ears are somewhat large holes in the sides of your bird's head. Cockatiels have about the same ability to distinguish sound waves and determine the location of the sound as people do, but birds seem to be less sensitive to higher and lower pitches than their owners.

Smell

You may be wondering how your pet's sense of smell compares to your own. Birds seem to have poorly developed senses of smell because smells often dissipate quickly in the air (where flying birds spend the majority of their time).

Touch

The final sense we relate to, touch, is well-developed in parrots. Parrots use their feet and their mouths to touch their surroundings (young birds particularly seem to "mouth" everything they can get their beaks on), to play and to determine what is safe to perch on or chew on and what's good to eat.

*Cockatiels' toe
arrangement, two
toes forward and
two toes back,
enables them to
use their feet for
balance.*

Along with their tactile uses, a parrot's feet also have an unusual design compared to other caged birds. Unlike a finch, the cockatiel's toes point forward and two point backward in an arrangement called zygodactyl, and it allows a parrot to climb up, down and around trees easily. Some larger parrots also use their feet to hold food or to play with toys.

Health Care

With good care, a cockatiel can live about twenty years, and some birds live well into their late twenties or thirties. One good example of cockatiel longevity was aviculturist Marie Olssen's bird, Bobbi, who was hatched in 1950 and died in 1985. At the time of his death, Bobbi was almost thirty-five years old! Unfortunately, the average life span of these small parrots is often much shorter. One of the reasons cockatiels don't live longer is that their owners may be reluctant to take their pets to the veterinarian. Some people don't want to pay veterinary bills on such "inexpensive" birds.

VISITING THE VETERINARIAN

As a caring owner, you want your bird to have the best chance at living a long, healthy life. To that end, you will need to locate a veterinarian who understands the special medical needs of birds with whom you can establish a good working relationship. The best time to do this is when you first bring your cockatiel home from the breeder or pet store. If possible, arrange to visit your veterinarian's office on your way home from the breeder or store. This is particularly important if you have other birds at home, because you don't want to endanger the health of your existing flock or your new pet.

Look for a veterinarian who has extensive education and experience in avian medicine.

If you don't know an avian veterinarian in your area, ask the person you bought your cockatiel from where he or she takes his or her birds.(Breeders and bird stores usually have avian veterinarians on whom they depend.) Talk to other bird owners you know and find out who they take their pets to, or call bird clubs in your area for referrals.

Another good source is the phone book, or yellow pages. Read the advertisements for veterinarians carefully, and try to find one who specializes in birds. Many veterinarians who have an interest in treating birds will join the Association of Avian Veterinarians and advertise themselves as members of this organization. Some veterinarians have taken and passed a special examination that entitles them to call themselves avian specialists.

The Physical Exam

After the question-and-answer session with you, the exam will begin. Your veterinarian will probably take his first look at your cockatiel while she is still in her cage or carrier. The veterinarian does this to give the bird an opportunity to become accustomed to him, rather than simply reaching right in and grabbing your pet. While the veterinarian is talking to you, he will check the bird's feather condition, her overall appearance, posture and perching ability.

Next, the doctor will drape a towel over his hand and gently catch your cockatiel and remove her from her carrier or cage. When the bird is out of her carrier, the doctor will look her over carefully. He will note the condition of your pet's eyes, her beak and her nares (nostrils). He will weigh your bird in a device that looks like a metal colander balanced on a scale, and the doctor will feel, or palpate, your bird's body, wings, legs and feet for any abnormalities.

Common Avian Tests

After your veterinarian has completed the physical examination, he may recommend further tests for your cockatiel. These can include:

- Blood workups, which can be further broken down into a complete blood count that determines how many platelets, red and white blood cells your bird has (this information can help diagnose infections or anemia), and a blood chemistry profile, which helps a veterinarian analyze how your bird's body processes enzymes, electrolytes and other chemicals.

- X-rays, which allow a veterinarian to study a bird's internal organs and bones. X-rays also help doctors find foreign bodies in a bird's system.

- Microbiological exams, which help determine if any unusual organisms (bacteria, fungi or yeast) are growing inside your bird's body.

- Fecal analysis, which studies a small sample of your bird's droppings to determine if she has internal parasites, or a bacterial or yeast infection.

Once the examination is concluded and you've had a chance to discuss any questions you have with your veterinarian, the doctor will probably recommend a follow-up examination schedule for your pet. Most healthy birds visit the veterinarian annually, but some have to go more frequently.

To help your veterinarian and to keep your pet from suffering long-term health risks, keep a close eye on her daily activities and appearance. If something suddenly changes in the way your bird looks or acts, contact your veterinarian immediately. Birds naturally hide signs of illness to protect themselves from predators, so by the time a bird looks or acts sick, it may already be dangerously ill.

MEDICATING YOUR COCKATIEL

Most bird owners will have to medicate their pets at some point in the birds' lives, and many are unsure if they can complete the task without hurting their birds. If you have to medicate your pet, your avian veterinarian or veterinary technician should explain the process to you. In the course of the explanation, you should find out how you will be administering the medication, how much of a given drug you will be giving your bird, how often the bird needs the medication and how long the entire course of treatment will last.

Be aware of your bird's normal activities. Changes can signal illness, and you'll want to take action right away.

If you find (as I often have) that you've forgotten one or more of these steps after you arrive home with your bird and your instructions, call your vet's office for clarification to ensure that your bird receives the follow-up care from you that she needs to recover.

Let's briefly review the most common methods of administering medications to birds, which are discussed completely in *The Complete Bird Owner's Handbook* by Gary A. Gallerstein, DVM. They are:

By mouth: This is a good route to take with birds that are small, easy to handle or underweight. The medication is usually given with a needleless plastic syringe placed in the left side of the bird's mouth and pointed toward the right side of her throat. This route is recommended to ensure that the medication gets into the bird's digestive system and not into her lungs, where aspiration pneumonia can result.

Medicating a bird's food or offering medicated feed (such as tetracyline-laced pellets that used to be fed to imported birds during quarantine to prevent psittacosis) is another effective possibility, but medications added to a bird's water supply are often less effective because sick birds are less likely to drink water, and the medicated water may have an unusual taste that makes a bird less likely to drink it.

By injection: Avian veterinarians consider this the most effective method of medicating birds. Some injection sites—into a vein, beneath the skin or into a bone—are used by avian veterinarians in the clinic setting. Bird owners are usually asked to medicate their birds intramuscularly, or by injecting medication into the bird's chest muscle. This is the area of the bird's body that has the greatest muscle mass, so it is a good injection site.

It's perfectly understandable if you're hesitant about giving your bird shots. Wrap your bird securely, but comfortably, in a washcloth or small towel, and lay her on your lap with her chest up. Hold her head securely with your thumb and index finger of one hand, and use the other to insert the syringe at about a 45-degree angle under the bird's chest feathers and into the muscle beneath.

You should remember to alternate the side you inject your bird on (say, left in the morning and right in the evening) to ensure that one side doesn't get overinjected and sore. Try to remain calm and talk to your bird in a soothing tone while you're adminis-tering the drugs. Before you both know it, the shot is over and your bird is one step closer to a complete recovery!

> ## SIGNS OF ILLNESS
>
> If your bird shows any of these signs, contact your veterinarian immediately for further instructions. Your bird should be seen as soon as possible.
>
> - a fluffed-up appearance
> - a loss of appetite
> - the bird wants to sleep all the time
> - a change in the appearance or number of droppings
> - weight loss
> - listlessness
> - drooping wings
> - lameness
> - the bird has partially eaten food stuck to her face or food has been regurgitated onto the cage floor
> - labored breathing, with or without tail bobbing
> - runny eyes or nose
> - the bird stops whistling or singing

Topical: This method, which is far less stressful than the one we just discussed, provides medication directly to part of a bird's body. Uses can include medications for eye infections, dry skin on the feet or legs or sinus problems.

Cockatiel Health Concerns

Although cockatiels are generally hardy birds, they are prone to a few health problems, including *Giardia*, conjunctivitis, candida, roundworms and papillomas. They, like all birds, can also suffer from respiratory problems and other conditions that result from a vitamin A deficiency, especially if they consume diets that are high in seeds and low in vitamin A–rich foods. Vitamin A deficiency can be prevented by feeding a varied, healthy diet.

GIARDIA

Giardia is caused by a protozoan called *Giardia psittaci*. Signs of a *Giardia* infection include loose droppings, weight loss, feather picking (especially under the wings), loss of appetite and depression. Your avian veterinarian may have difficulty diagnosing this disease because the *Giardia* organism is difficult to detect in a bird's feces. The disease can be spread through contaminated food or water, and birds are not immune to it once they've had it. Your veterinarian can recommend an appropriate medication to treat *Giardia*.

In some birds, a *Giardia* infection can lead to other problems, such as cockatiel paralysis syndrome, which is seen most often in lutino birds that are infected with *Giardia* or *Hexamita*. It's caused by a vitamin E/selenium deficiency. Signs include slow eye blink, weak jaw muscles, poor digestion, clumsiness and a weak grip, spraddle leg, weak hatchlings, an increase in the number of dead-in-shell chicks and decreased fertility. Antiprotozoal therapy and supplemental vitamin E/selenium have successfully treated the condition.

CONJUNCTIVITIS

Cockatiel conjunctivitis is seen in white or albino birds more than in normal grays. Signs include inflammation of the eyelid and discharge from the eye with no apparent cause. Treatment with topical antibiotic ointment resolves the signs temporarily, but recurrences are common. Affected birds should not be used in breeding programs because there is some evidence that this is a genetic problem.

Healthy cockatiels have clear eyes that are free of discharge.

CANDIDA

Cockatiel breeders need to pay particular attention to candida, which is caused by the yeast *Candida albicans.* Young cockatiels seem to be particularly susceptible to candida infestations, which occur when a bird's diet is low in vitamin A. Signs of candida include white, cheesy growths in the bird's mouth and throat; a loss of appetite; regurgitation or vomiting; and a crop that is slow to empty.

The trouble with trying to diagnose a candida infestation is that many adult cockatiels don't show any signs of the condition, so a breeder may not even know he or she has infected birds until the parent birds pass the yeast to the chicks during feeding. Hand-fed chicks are not immune to the condition, either, because they can be affected by it if their throats are damaged by feeding tubes. Veterinary assistance in the form of antifungal drugs and a diet high in vitamin A may be your best weapons against candida.

ROUNDWORMS

Roundworms, or ascarids, can infest cockatiels that have access to dirt, which is where roundworm eggs are found. The worms themselves are two to five inches long and resemble white spaghetti. Mild infestations of roundworms can cause weight loss, appetite loss, growth abnormalities and diarrhea, while heavy infestations can result in bowel blockage and death.

To diagnose roundworms, your veterinarian will analyze a sample of your bird's droppings. He or she can then prescribe an appropriate course of treatment to clear up the problem.

A baseline measurement of weight should be taken on your cockatiel's first visit to the veterinarian. This will be useful later if you suspect that your bird is ill.

Raccoon roundworms, which are passed in the animal's feces, can also affect cockatiels. To protect birds from this parasite, which can cause damage to a bird's central nervous system, prevent raccoons from accessing your aviaries.

SARCOCYSTIS

Another parasite problem, sarcocystis, can be a problem in North American areas with large opossum populations. Sarcocystis infections seem more prevalent in the winter months, and male birds are more susceptible to this parasite than females. Birds affected by sarcocystis often appear healthy one day and are dead the next. Those birds that do show signs of illness before dying become lethargic, cannot breathe easily and pass yellowish droppings. As with the raccoon roundworms, preventing opossums from accessing your aviaries can eliminate the threat of this disease. However, cockroaches can also pass along this parasite by consuming opossum feces and then being eaten by an aviary cockatiel.

PAPILLOMAS

Papillomas are benign tumors that can appear almost anywhere on a bird's skin, including its foot, leg, eyelid or preen gland. If a bird has a papilloma on her cloaca, the bird may appear to have a "wet raspberry" coming out of her vent. These tumors, which are caused by a virus, can appear as small, crusty lesions, or they may be raised growths that have a bumpy texture or small projections.

Many papillomas can be left untreated without harm to the bird, but some must be removed by an avian veterinarian because a bird may pick at the growth and cause it to bleed.

BALD SPOTS

Although it isn't a health problem per se, some cockatiels, particularly lutinos, are prone to bald spots behind their crests. These spots resulted from inbreeding cockatiels to create the mutation in the 1950s. Birds with noticeable bald spots on the backs of their heads are generally held out of breeding programs to try to ensure that the trait doesn't get passed on to future generations.

OTHER AVIAN HEALTH CONDITIONS

Polyomavirus, which is sometimes called French moult, causes flight and tail feathers to develop improperly or not develop at all. Polyomavirus can be spread through contact with new birds, as well as from feather and fecal dust.

Adult birds can carry polyomavirus but not show any signs of the disease. These seemingly healthy birds can pass the virus to young birds that have never been exposed, and these young birds can die from polyomavirus rather quickly. Sick birds can become weak, lose their appetites, bleed beneath the skin, have enlarged abdomens, become paralyzed, regurgitate and have diarrhea. Some birds with polyomavirus suddenly die.

At present, there is no cure, although a vaccine is under development. Protecting your pets against polyomavirus and other diseases is why it's important to quarantine new stock and to take precautions, including showering and changing clothes, before handling your pet when you've gone to other bird owners' homes, to bird marts that have large numbers of birds from different vendors on display or to bird specialty stores with unhealthy stock.

Psittacine beak and feather disease syndrome (PBFDS) has been a hot topic among birdkeepers for the last decade. The virus was first detected in cockatoos and was originally thought to be a cockatoo-specific problem. It has since been determined that more than forty species of parrots, including cockatiels, can contract this disease, which causes a bird's feathers to become pinched or clubbed in appear-ance. Other symptoms include beak fractures and mouth ulcers. This highly contagious, fatal disease is most common in birds less than three years of age, and there is no cure at present. A vaccine is under development at the University of Georgia.

WHAT TO AVOID

In The Complete Bird Owner's Handbook, veterinarian Gary Gallerstein offers the following "don'ts" to bird owners whose birds need urgent care:

- Don't give a bird human medications or medications prescribed for another animal unless so directed by your veterinarian.

- Don't give your bird medications that are suggested by a friend, a store employee or a human physician.

- Don't give a bird alcohol or laxatives.

- Don't apply any oils or ointments to your bird unless your veterinarian tells you to do so.

- Don't bathe a sick bird.

Cockatiel First Aid

Sometimes your pet will get itself into a situation that will require quick thinking and even quicker action on your part to help save your bird from serious injury or death. I'd like to outline some basic first aid techniques that may prove to be useful in these situations.

BASIC SUPPLIES

Before we get into the specific techniques, I'd like to suggest that you assemble a bird owner's first aid kit so that you will have some basic supplies on hand before your bird needs them. Here's what to include:

- appropriate-sized towels for catching and holding your bird

- a heating pad, heat lamp or other heat source

- a pad of paper and pencil to make notes about bird's condition

- styptic powder, silver nitrate stick or cornstarch to stop bleeding (use styptic powder and silver nitrate stick on beak and nails only)

- blunt-tipped scissors

- nail clippers and nail file

- needle-nosed pliers to pull broken blood feathers

- blunt-end tweezers

- hydrogen peroxide or other disinfectant solution

- eye irrigation solution

- bandage materials such as gauze squares, masking tape (it doesn't stick to a bird's feathers like adhesive tape does) and gauze rolls

- Pedialyte or other energy supplement

- eye dropper

- syringes to irrigate wounds or feed sick birds

- penlight

Keep all these supplies in one place, such as a fishing tackle box. This will eliminate having to search for supplies in emergency situations, and the case can be taken along to bird shows, on trips or left for the bird-sitter.

FIRST, STABILIZE

No matter what the situation, there are a few things to keep in mind when facing a medical emergency with your pet. First, keep as calm as possible to lessen the shock of injury and to reassure your pet. Next, stop any bleeding, keep the bird warm and minimize handling her.

After you've stabilized your pet, call your veterinarian's office for further instructions. Tell them "This is an emergency" and that your bird has had an accident. Describe what happened to your pet as clearly and calmly as you can. Listen carefully to the instructions you are given and follow them. Finally, transport your bird to the vet's office as quickly and safely as you can.

Your calm demeanor will soothe and decrease the stress of an ill or injured cockatiel.

Urgent Medical Situations

Here are some urgent medical situations that bird owners are likely to encounter, the reason that they are medical emergencies, the signs and symptoms your bird might show, and the recommended treatments for the problem:

ANIMAL BITES

It's an emergency because: infections can develop from bacteria on the biting animal's teeth and/or claws. Also, a bird's internal organs can be damaged by the bite.

Signs: Sometimes the bite marks can be seen, but often the bird shows few, if any, signs of injury.

Steps to take: Call your veterinarian's office and transport the bird there immediately. Treatment for shock and antibiotics are often the course of action veterinarians take to save birds that have been bitten.

BEAK INJURY

It's an emergency because: a bird needs both her upper and lower beak (also called the upper and lower mandible) to eat and preen properly. Infections can also set in rather quickly if a beak is fractured or punctured.

Signs: Bird is bleeding from her beak. This often occurs after the bird flies into a windowpane or mirror, or if she has a run-in with an operational ceiling fan. Bird may have also cracked or damaged her beak, and portions of the beak may be missing.

Steps to take: Control bleeding. Keep bird calm and quiet. Contact your avian veterinarian's office.

BLEEDING

It's an emergency because: a bird can withstand only about a 20 percent loss of blood volume and still recover from an injury.

Signs: In the event of external bleeding, you will see blood on the bird, her cage and her surroundings. In the case of internal bleeding, the bird may pass bloody droppings or bleed from her nose, mouth or vent.

Steps to take: For external bleeding, apply direct pressure. If the bleeding doesn't stop with direct pressure, apply a coagulant, such as styptic powder (for nails and beaks) or cornstarch (for broken feathers and skin injuries). If the bleeding stops, observe the bird for restarting of the bleeding or for shock. Call your veterinarian's office if the bird seems weak or if she has lost a lot of blood and arrange to take the bird in for further treatment.

Broken blood feathers can result in bleeding. Blood feathers can break horizontally (across the feather) or vertically (along the feather shaft). Horizontal breaks are more common, and they often result from a bird pulling at a blood feather or an owner accidentally cutting a blood feather while trimming a bird's wings.

In severe cases that do not respond to direct pressure, you may have to remove the feather shaft to stop the bleeding. To do this, grasp the feather shaft as close to the skin as you can with a pair of needle-nosed pliers and pull out the shaft with a swift, steady motion. Apply direct pressure to the skin after you remove the feather shaft.

BREATHING PROBLEMS

It's an emergency because: Respiratory problems in pet birds can be life threatening.

Signs: The bird wheezes or clicks while breathing, bobs her tail, breathes with an open mouth, has discharge from her nares or swelling around her eyes.

Steps to take: Keep the bird warm, place her in a bathroom with a hot shower running to help her breathe easier and call your veterinarian's office.

BURNS

It's an emergency because: Birds that are burned severely enough can go into shock and may die.

Signs: A burned bird has reddened skin and burnt or greasy feathers. The bird may also show signs of shock (see below for details).

Steps to take: Mist burned area with cool water. Apply antibiotic cream or spray lightly. **Do not apply any oily or greasy substances,** including butter. If the bird seems to be in shock or the burn is widespread, contact your veterinarian's office for further instructions.

CONCUSSION

It's an emergency because: A concussion results from a sharp blow to the head that can cause injury to the brain.

Signs: Birds sometimes suffer concussions when they fly into mirrors or windows. They will seem stunned and may go into shock.

Steps to take: Keep the bird warm, prevent her from hurting herself further and watch her carefully. Alert your veterinarian's office to the injury.

CLOACAL PROLAPSE

It's an emergency because: The bird's lower intestines, uterus or cloaca is protruding from the bird's vent.

Signs: The bird has pink, red, brown or black tissue protruding from her vent.

Steps to take: Contact your veterinarian's office for immediate follow-up care. Your veterinarian can usually reposition the organs.

EGG BINDING

It's an emergency because: The egg blocks the hen's excretory system and makes it impossible for her to eliminate. Also, eggs can sometimes break inside the hen, which can lead to infection.

Signs: An egg-bound hen strains to lay eggs unsuccessfully. She becomes fluffed and lethargic, sits on the floor of her cage, may be paralyzed and may have a swollen abdomen.

Steps to take: Keep the hen warm as this sometimes helps her pass the egg. Put her and her cage into a warm bathroom with a hot shower running to increase the humidity, which may also help her pass the egg. If your bird doesn't improve shortly (within a hour), contact your veterinarian.

EYE INJURY

It's an emergency because: Untreated eye problems may lead to blindness.

Signs: Swollen or pasty eyelids, discharge, cloudy eyeball, increased rubbing of eye area.

Steps to take: Examine the eye carefully for foreign bodies. Contact your veterinarian for more information.

FRACTURES

It's an emergency because: A fracture can cause a bird to go into shock. Depending on the type of fracture, infections can also set in.

Signs: Birds most often break bones in their legs, so be on the lookout for a bird that is holding one leg at an odd angle or that isn't putting weight on one leg. Sudden swelling of a leg or wing, or a droopy wing can also indicate fractures.

Steps to take: Confine the bird to her cage or a small carrier. Don't handle her unnecessarily. Keep her warm and contact your veterinarian.

FROSTBITE

It's an emergency because: A bird could lose toes or feet to frostbite. She could also go into shock and die as a result.

Signs: The frostbitten area is very cold and dry to the touch and is pale in color.

Steps to take: Warm the damaged tissue up gradually in a circulating water bath. Keep bird warm and contact your veterinarian's office for further instructions.

INHALED OR EATEN FOREIGN OBJECT

It's an emergency because: Birds can develop serious respiratory or digestive problems from foreign objects in their bodies.

Signs: In the case of inhaled items, wheezing and other respiratory problems. In the case of consumed objects, the bird was seen playing with a small item that suddenly cannot be found.

Steps to take: If you suspect that your bird has inhaled or eaten something she shouldn't, contact your veterinarian's office immediately.

Lead Poisoning

It's an emergency because: Birds can die from lead poisoning.

Signs: A bird with lead poisoning may act depressed or weak. She may be blind, or she may walk in circles at the bottom of her cage. She may regurgitate or pass droppings that resemble tomato juice.

Steps to take: Contact your avian veterinarian immediately. Lead poisoning requires a quick start to treatment, and the treatment may require several days or weeks to complete successfully.

Note: Lead poisoning is easily prevented by keeping birds away from common sources of lead in the home. These include stained glass items, leaded paint found in some older homes, fishing weights, drapery weights and parrot toys (some are weighted with lead). One item that won't cause lead poisoning are "lead" pencils (they're actually graphite).

Overheating

It's an emergency because: High body temperatures can kill a bird.

Signs: An overheated bird will try to make herself thin. She will hold her wings away from her body, open her mouth and roll her tongue in an attempt to cool herself. Birds don't have sweat glands, so they must try to cool their bodies by exposing as much of their skin's surface as they can to moving air.

Steps to take: Cool the bird off by putting her in front of a fan (make sure the blades are screened so the bird doesn't injure itself further), by spraying her with cool water or by having her stand in a bowl of cool water. Let the bird drink cool water if she can (if she can't, offer her cool water with an eyedropper) and contact your veterinarian.

Poisoning

It's an emergency because: Poisons can kill a bird quickly.

Signs: Poisoned birds may suddenly regurgitate, have diarrhea or bloody droppings and have redness or burns around their mouths. They may also go into convulsions, become paralyzed or go into shock.

Steps to take: Put the poison out of your bird's reach. Contact your veterinarian for further instructions. Be prepared to take the poison with you to the vet's office in case he or she needs to contact a poison control center for further information.

SEIZURES

It's an emergency because: Seizures can indicate a number of serious conditions, including lead poisoning, infections, nutritional deficiency, heat stroke and epilepsy.

Signs: The bird goes into a seizure that lasts from a few seconds to a minute. Afterward, she seems dazed and may stay on the cage floor for several hours. She may also appear unsteady and won't perch.

Steps to take: Keep the bird from hurting herself further by removing everything you can from her cage. Cover the bird's cage with a towel and darken the room to reduce the bird's stress level. Contact your veterinarian's office for further instructions immediately.

SHOCK

It's an emergency because: Shock indicates that the bird's circulatory system cannot move the blood supply around the bird's body. This is a serious condition that can lead to death if left untreated.

Signs: Shocky birds may act depressed, breathe rapidly and have a fluffed appearance. If your bird displays these signs in conjunction with a recent accident, suspect shock and take appropriate action.

Steps to take: Keep your bird warm, cover her cage and transport her to your veterinarian's office as soon as possible.

Veterinarian Michael Murray recommends that bird owners keep the following tips in mind when facing emergency situations:

Keep the bird warm. You can do this by putting the bird in an empty aquarium with a heating pad under her, by putting a heat lamp near the bird's cage or by putting a heating pad set on low under the bird's cage in place of the cage tray. Whatever heat source you choose to use, make sure to keep a close eye on your bird so that she doesn't accidentally burn herself on the pad or lamp and that she doesn't chew on a power cord.

Put the bird in a dark, quiet room. This helps reduce the bird's stress.

Put the bird's food in locations that are easy to reach. Sick birds need to eat, but they may not be able to reach food in its normal locations in the cage. Sometimes, birds require hand-feeding to keep their calorie consumption steady.

Protect the bird from additional injury. If the convalescing bird is in a clear-sided aquarium, for example, you may want to put a towel over the glass to keep the bird from flying into it.

Preventive Care

Your cockatiel requires a certain level of care each day to ensure her health and well-being. Here are some of the things you'll need to do each day for your pet:

- Observe your pet for any changes in her routine (report any changes to your avian veterinarian immediately).

- Offer fresh food and remove old food. Wash food dish thoroughly with detergent and water. Rinse thoroughly and allow to dry.

- Check seed dish and refill as necessary with clean, fresh seed.

- Provide fresh water and remove previous dish. Wash dish as above.

- Change paper in cage tray.

- Let the bird out of her cage for supervised playtime.

- Finally, you'll want to cover your bird's cage at about the same time every night to indicate bedtime.

Cockatiels, like all parrots, seem to enjoy a familiar routine. When you cover the cage, you'll probably hear your bird rustling around for a bit, perhaps getting a drink of water or a last mouthful of seeds before settling in for the night. Keep in mind that your pet will require eight to ten hours of sleep a day, but you can expect that she will take naps during the day to supplement her nightly snooze.

MONITOR DROPPINGS

Taking good care of your cockatiel will help bond you with your bird.

Although it may seem a bit unpleasant to discuss, your bird's droppings require daily monitoring because they can tell you a lot about her general health. Cockatiels produce white-and-green tubular drop-

pings. These droppings are usually composed of equal amounts of fecal material (the green portion), urine (a clear liquid portion) and urates (the white or cream-colored part). A healthy cockatiel generally eliminates about every fifteen minutes, although your bird may go more or less often.

Texture and consistency, along with frequency or lack of droppings, can let you know how your pet is feeling. For instance, if a bird eats a lot of fruits and vegetables, her droppings are generally looser and more watery than a bird that eats primarily seeds. But watery droppings can also indicate illness, such as diabetes or kidney problems, that cause a bird to drink more water than usual.

Color can also give an indication of health. Birds that have psittacosis typically have bright, lime-green droppings, while healthy birds have avocado or darker green and white droppings. Birds with liver problems may produce droppings that are yellowish or reddish, while birds that have internal bleeding will produce dark, tarry droppings.

A color change doesn't necessarily indicate poor health in your cockatiel. For instance, birds that eat pelleted diets tend to have darker droppings than their seed-eating companions, while parrots that have splurged on a certain fresh food soon have droppings with that characteristic color. Birds that overindulge on beets, for instance, produce bright red droppings that can look for all the world as though the bird has suffered some serious internal injury. Other birds that overdo sweet potatoes, blueberries or raspberries produce orange, blue or red droppings. During pomegranate season, birds that enjoy this fruit develop violet droppings that can look alarming to an unprepared owner.

As part of your daily cage cleaning and observation of your feathered friend, look at her droppings carefully. Learn what is normal for your bird in terms of color, consistency and frequency, and report any changes to your avian veterinarian promptly.

Weekly Chores

The following chores should be done on a weekly basis to keep your cockatiel healthy and happy:

- Removing old food from cage bars and from the corners of the cage where it invariably falls.

- Removing, scraping and replacing the perches to keep them clean and free of debris (you might also want to sand them lightly with coarse grain sandpaper to clean them further and improve perch traction for your bird).

- Rotating toys in your bird's cage to keep them interesting. Remember to discard any toys that show excessive signs of wear (frayed rope, cracked plastic or well-chewed wood).

Cage Cleaning Tips

You can simplify the weekly cage cleaning process by placing the cage in the shower and letting hot water from the shower head do some of the work. Be sure to remove your bird, her food and water dishes, the cage tray paper and her toys before putting the cage into the shower. You can let the hot water run over the cage for a few minutes, then scrub at any stuck-on food with an old toothbrush or some fine-grade steel wool. After you've removed the food and other debris, you can disinfect the cage with a spray-on disinfectant that you can purchase at your pet store. Make sure to choose a bird-safe product, and read the instructions completely before use.

Rinse the cage thoroughly and dry it completely before returning your bird and her accessories to the cage. (If you have wooden perches in the cage, you can dry them more quickly by placing the wet dowels in a 400-degree oven for 10 minutes. Let the perches cool before you put them back in the cage.)

Regulate Temperature

Warm weather requires a little extra vigilance on the part of a pet bird owner to ensure that your pet remains comfortable even in hot weather. To help keep your pet cool, keep her out of direct sun, offer her lots of fresh, juicy vegetables and fruits (be sure to remove these fresh foods from the cage promptly to prevent your bird from eating spoiled food) and mist her lightly with a clean spray bottle (filled with water only) that is used solely for showering your bird.

By the same token, pay attention to your pet's needs when the weather turns cooler. You may want to use a heavier cage cover, especially if you lower the heat in your home at bedtime, or you may want to move the bird's cage to another location in your home that is

warmer and less drafty.

About Molting

At least once a year, your cockatiel will lose her feathers. Don't be alarmed, because this is a normal process called molting. Many pet birds seem to be in a perpetual molt, with feathers falling out and coming in throughout the summer.

You can consider your bird in molting season when you see a lot of whole feathers in the bottom of the cage and you notice that your bird seems to have broken out in a rash of stubby little aglets (like those plastic tips on the ends of your shoelaces). These are the feather sheaths that help new pinfeathers break through the skin, and they are made of keratin (the same material that makes up our fingernails). The sheaths also help protect growing feathers from damage until the feather completes its growth cycle.

You may notice that your cockatiel is a little more irritable during the molt; this is to be expected. Think about how you would feel if you had all these itchy new feathers coming in all of a sudden. However, your bird may actively seek out more time with you during the molt because owners are handy to have around when a cockatiel has an itch on the top of her head that she can't quite scratch! (Scratch these new feathers gently because some of them may still be growing in and may be sensitive to the touch.) Some birds may benefit from special conditioning foods during the molt; check with your avian veterinarian to see if your bird is a candidate for these foods.

> **COMFORT DURING MOLTING**
>
> - encourage balanced nutrition
> - decrease stress by emphasizing security and rest periods
> - keep room temperature between 75° and 80° F during heavy shedding
> - promote preening activity

Enjoying

Your

Cockatiel

Understanding
Your
Cockatiel

Most new bird owners have high expectations for developing a loving relationship with their pet. The goal is to nurture a relationship with your cockatiel that will result in a bird who will interact well with people, be pleasant company and show little sign of aggressiveness (such as screaming). Sometimes, however, we forget that birds in captivity are not in their natural surroundings and can't always live up to our expectations. Having knowledge, understanding and respect for your pet's behavior characteristics will foster a trusting and happy relationship.

Basic Cockatiel Behavior

The following common avian behaviors are listed in alphabetical order to help you better understand your new feathered friend!

As your cockatiel becomes more settled in your home, don't be surprised if you hear subtle little fluffs coming from under the cage cover first thing in the morning. It's as if your bird is saying, "I hear that you're up. I'm up, too. Don't forget to uncover me and play with me!" Other attention-getting behaviors include gently shaking toys, sneezing or soft vocalizations.

Beak Grinding

If you hear your bird making odd little grinding noises as he's drifting off to sleep, don't be alarmed! Beak grinding is a sign of a contented pet bird, and it's commonly heard as a bird settles in for the night.

Stretching the wings is a common behavior in cockatiels, and sure feels good!

Beak Wiping

After a meal, it's common for a cockatiel to wipe his beak against a perch or on the cage floor to clean it.

Birdie Aerobics

This is how I describe a sudden bout of stretching that all parrots seem prone to. An otherwise calm bird will suddenly grab the cage bars and stretch the wing and leg muscles on one side of his body, or he will raise both wings in imitation of an eagle.

Catnaps

You will probably catch your cockatiel taking a little catnap during the day. These active little birds seem to be either going full-tilt, playing and eating, or catching a few Zs. As long as you see no other indications of illness, such as a loss of appetite or a fluffed-up appearance, there is no need to worry if your pet sleeps during the day.

FEATHER PICKING

Don't confuse this with preening (see below). Feather picking results from physical causes, such as a dietary imbalance, a hormonal change, a thyroid problem or an infection of the skin or feathers. It can also be caused by emotional upset, such as a change in the owner's appearance, a change in the bird's routine, another pet being added to the home, a new baby in the home or a number of other factors. Once feather picking begins, it may be difficult to get a bird to stop. Although it looks painful to us, some birds find the routine of pulling out their feathers emotionally soothing. Cockatiels that suddenly begin picking their feathers, especially those under the wings, may have an intestinal parasite called *Giardia*. If you notice that your bird suddenly starts pulling his feathers out, contact your avian veterinarian for an evaluation.

FLUFFING

This is often a prelude to preening or a tension releaser. If your bird fluffs up, stays fluffed and resembles a little feathered pine cone, however, contact your avian veterinarian for an appointment because fluffed feathers can be an indicator of illness.

HISSING

If your cockatiel hisses, it's because he is frightened of something in his environment that he's trying to scare away by hissing.

MUTUAL PREENING

This is part of the preening behavior described below, and it can take place between birds or between birds and their owners. It is a sign of affection reserved for best friends or mates, so consider it an honor if your cockatiel wants to preen your eyebrows, hair, mustache or beard, or your arms and hands.

PAIR BONDING

This is discussed in the context of breeding later in the book, but I wanted to include it here, too, to point out that not only mated pairs bond, but best bird buddies of the same sex will demonstrate some of the same behavior, including sitting close to each other, preening each other and mimicking the other's actions, such as stretching or scratching, often at the same time.

POSSESSIVENESS

Cockatiels can become overly attached to one person in the household, especially if that same person is the one who is primarily responsible for their care. Indications of a possessive cockatiel can include hissing and other threatening gestures made toward other family members, and pair bonding behavior with the chosen family member. You can keep your cockatiel from becoming possessive by having all members of the family spend time with your bird from the time you first bring it home. Encourage different members of the family to feed the bird and clean his cage, and make sure all family members play with the bird and socialize him while he's out of his cage.

If your cockatiel wants to be preened, he will tell you by approaching you with his head down and gently nudging you where he wants to be scratched and petted.

PREENING

This is part of a cockatiel's normal routine. You will see your bird ruffling and straightening his feathers each day. He will also take oil from the uropygial or preen gland at the base of his tail and put the oil on the rest of his feathers, so don't be concerned if you see your pet seeming to peck or bite at his tail. If, during molting, your bird seems to remove whole feathers, don't panic! Old, worn feathers are pushed out by incoming new ones, which makes the old feathers loose and easy to remove.

REGURGITATING

If you see that your bird is pinning his eyes (pupils enlarge, then contract, then enlarge again), bobbing his head and pumping his neck and crop muscles, he is about to regurgitate some food for you. Birds regurgitate to their mates during breeding season and to their young while raising chicks. It is a mark of great affection to have your bird regurgitate his dinner for you, so try not to be too disgusted if your pet starts bringing up his last meal for you.

RESTING ON ONE FOOT

Do not be alarmed if you see your cockatiel occasionally resting on only one foot. This is normal behavior (the resting foot is often drawn up into the belly feathers). If you see your bird always using both feet to perch, please contact your avian veterinarian because this can indicate a health problem.

SCREAMING

Well-cared-for cockatiels will vocalize quietly (see separate entry for vocalization), but birds that feel neglected and that have little attention paid to them may become screamers. Once a bird becomes a screamer, it can be a difficult habit to break, particularly since the bird feels rewarded with your negative

LEARN TO READ A COCKATIEL'S MOOD BY ITS CREST

Here's what to look for:

- Content cockatiels keep their crests lowered. Only the tips of the feathers point upward.

- Playful, alert cockatiels raise their crests vertically. This position indicates that the bird is ready for action.

- Agitated cockatiels raise their crests straight up and have the feather tips leaning forward slightly.

- Frightened cockatiels whip their crests back and hiss in a threatening manner. They also stand tall, ready to fight or take flight as the situation dictates.

attention every time he screams. You may not see your attention as a reward, but at least the bird gets to see you and to hear from you as you tell him (often in a loud, dramatic way) to be quiet.

Remember to give your bird consistent attention (at least 30 minutes a day); provide him with an interesting environment, complete with a variety of toys, a well-balanced diet; and leave a radio or television on when you're away to provide background noise, and your bird shouldn't become a screamer.

SNEEZING

In pet birds, sneezes are classified as either nonproductive or productive. Nonproductive sneezes clear a bird's nares (what we think of as nostrils) and are nothing to worry about. Some birds even stick a claw into their nares to induce a sneeze from time to time, much as a snuff dipper takes a pinch to produce the same effect. Productive sneezes, on the other hand, produce a discharge and are a cause for concern. If your bird sneezes frequently and you see a discharge from his nares or notice the area around his nares is wet, contact your avian veterinarian immediately to set up an appointment to have your bird's health checked.

A playful cock-atiel will have an alert, inquisitive demeanor.

STRESS

This can show itself in many ways in your bird's behavior, including shaking, diarrhea, rapid breathing, wing and tail fanning, screaming, feather picking, poor sleeping habits or loss of appetite. Over a period of time, stress can harm your cockatiel's health. To

89

prevent your bird from becoming stressed, try to provide him with as normal and regular a routine as possible. Parrots are, for the most part, creatures of habit, and they don't always adapt well to sudden changes in their environment or schedule. But if you do have to change something, talk to your parrot about it first. I know it seems crazy, but telling your bird what you're going to do before you do it may actually help reduce his stress. I received this advice from avian behaviorist Christine Davis, and I explain what I'm doing every time I rearrange the living room on my bird or when I have had to leave her at the vet's office for boarding during business trips. If you're going to be away on vacation, tell your bird how long you'll be gone, and count the days out on your fingers in front of the bird or show him a calendar.

TASTING/TESTING THINGS WITH THE BEAK

Birds use their beaks and mouths to explore their world in much the same way people use their hands. For example, don't be surprised if your cockatiel reaches out to tentatively taste or bite your hand before stepping onto it the first time. Your bird isn't biting you to be mean; he's merely investigating his world and testing the strength of a new perch using the tools he has available.

THRASHING

Cockatiels, particularly lutinos, seem prone to a condition that is described as "night frights," "cockatiel thrashing syndrome" or "earthquake syndrome." Birds that experience thrashing episodes will be startled from sleep by loud noises or vibrations that cause a bird to awaken suddenly and try to take flight. In the case of caged pet birds, the thrasher may injure his wing tips, feet, chest or abdomen on toys or cage bars when he tries to flee from the perceived danger.

Bird owners can help protect their pets from harm by installing a small night-light near the bird's cage to help the bird see where he is during a thrashing episode, by placing an air cleaner in the bird's room to provide "white noise" that will drown out some potentially frightening background noises or by placing the bird in a small sleeping cage that is free of toys and other items that could harm a frightened bird.

THREATS

If your cockatiel wants to threaten a cagemate, another pet in the home or one of his human companions, he will stand as tall as he can with his crest raised halfway and his mouth open. He will also try to bite the object of his threats.

VOCALIZATION

Many parrots vocalize around sunrise and sunset, which I believe hearkens back to flock behavior in the wild when parrots call to each other to start and end their days. You may notice

It is natural and healthy for your cockatiel to display aggressive behavior if he senses a threat.

that your pet cockatiel calls to you when you are out of the room. This may mean that he feels lonely or that he needs some reassurance from you. Tell him that he's fine and that he's being a good bird, and the bird should settle down and begin playing or eating. If he continues to call to you, however, you may want to check on him to ensure that everything is all right in his world.

Household Hazards

The phrase "Curiosity killed the cat" could easily be rewritten to reflect a cockatiel's curious nature. These inquisitive little birds seem to be able to get into just about anything, which means they can get themselves into potentially dangerous situations rather quickly. Because of this natural curiosity, cockatiel owners must be extremely vigilant when their birds are out of their cages.

Part of this vigilance should include bird-proofing your home. Remember that some of the larger parrots are intellectually on a similar level as a toddler. You wouldn't let a toddler have free run of your house without taking a few precautions to safeguard the child from harm, and you should extend the same concern to your pet birds.

Make sure that the room your cockatiel is exploring has been "bird-proofed" for safety.

Let's go room by room and look at some of the potentially dangerous situations you should be aware of.

BATHROOM

This can be a cockatiel paradise if the bird is allowed to spend time with you as you prepare for work or for an evening out, but it can also be quite harmful to your bird's health. An open toilet could lead to the cockatiel drowning, the bird could hurt himself chewing on the cord of your blow-dryer or he could be overcome by fumes from perfume, hairspray or cleaning products, such as bleach, air freshener or toilet bowl cleaner. The bird could also become ill if he nibbles on prescription or nonprescription drugs in the medicine chest or he could injure himself by flying into a mirror. Use caution when taking your bird into the bathroom, and make sure his wings are clipped to avoid flying accidents.

KITCHEN

This is another popular spot for birds and their owners to hang out, especially around mealtime. Here again, dangers lurk for curious cockatiels. An unsupervised bird could fly or fall into the trash can, or he could climb into the oven, dishwasher, freezer or refrigerator and be forgotten. Your bird could also land on a hot stove element, or fall into an uncovered pot of boiling water, or sizzling frying pan on the stove. The bird could also become poisoned by eating foods that are unsafe for him, such as chocolate, avocado or rhubarb.

LIVING ROOM

Are you sitting on your couch or in a comfortable chair as you read this book? Although it probably seems safe enough to you, your pet could be injured or killed if he decided to play hide-and-seek under pillows or cushions and was accidentally sat on. Your cockatiel could become poisoned by nibbling on a leaded glass lampshade, or he could fly out an open window or patio door. By the same token, he could fly into a closed window or door and injure himself severely. He could become entangled in a drapery cord or a venetian blind pull, he could fall into an uncovered fish tank and drown or he could ingest poison by nibbling on ashes or used cigarette butts in an ashtray.

HOME OFFICE

This can be another cockatiel playground, but you'll have to be on your toes to keep your pet from harming himself by nibbling on potentially poisonous markers, glue sticks or crayons, or impaling himself on push pins.

OTHER AREAS OF CONCERN

If you have a ceiling fan in your house, make sure it is turned off when your bird is out of his cage. Make sure you know where your bird is before turning on your washer or dryer, and don't close your basement freezer without checking first to be sure your bird isn't in there.

This doesn't mean to keep your bird locked up in his cage all the time. On the contrary, all parrots need time out of their cages to maintain physical and mental health. The key is to be aware of some of the dangers that may exist in your home and to pay attention to your bird's behavior so you can intervene before the bird becomes ill or injured.

Unfortunately, potential dangers to a pet bird don't stop with the furniture and accessories. A variety of fumes can overpower your cockatiel, such as those from cigarettes, air fresheners, insecticides, bleach, shoe polish, oven cleaners, kerosene, lighter fluid, glues, active self-cleaning ovens, hairspray, overheated nonstick cookware, paint thinner, bathroom cleaners or nail polish remover. Try to keep your pet away from anything that has a strong chemical odor, and be sure to apply makeup and hair care products far away from your pet.

To help protect your pet from harmful chemical fumes, consider using some "green" cleaning alternatives, such as baking soda and vinegar to clear clogged

POISONOUS HOUSEPLANTS

- amaryllis
- bird of paradise
- calla lily
- daffodil
- dieffenbachia
- English ivy
- foxglove
- holly
- juniper
- lily-of-the-valley
- mistletoe
- oleander
- philodendron
- rhododendron
- rhubarb
- sweet pea
- wisteria

drains, baking soda instead of scouring powder to clean tubs and sinks, lemon juice and mineral oil to polish furniture and white vinegar and water as a window cleaner. These products keep the environment a little friendlier for your bird, and these simple solutions to cleaning problems often work better than higher-priced, name-brand products.

If you're considering a remodeling or home improvement project, think about your cockatiel first. Fumes from paint or formaldehyde, which can be found in carpet backing, paneling and particle board, can cause pets and people to become ill. If you are having work done on your home, consider boarding your cockatiel at your avian veterinarian's office or at the home of a bird-loving friend or relative until the project is complete and the house is aired out. You can consider the house safe for your pet when you cannot smell any trace of any of the products used in the remodeling.

Having your home fumigated for termites poses another potentially hazardous situation to your pet cockatiel. Ask your exterminator for information about the types of chemicals that will be used in your home, and inquire if pet-safe formulas, such as electrical currents or liquid nitrogen, are available. If your house must be treated chemically, arrange to board your bird at your avian veterinarian's office or with a friend before, during and after the fumigation to ensure that no harm comes to your pet. Make sure your house is aired out completely before bringing your bird home, too.

SAFE HOUSEPLANTS

- African violets
- aloe
- burro's tail
- Christmas cactus
- coleus
- edible fig
- fern (asparagus, Boston, bird's nest, maidenhair, ribbon, staghorn, squirrel's foot)
- gardenia
- grape ivy
- hen and chicks
- hibiscus
- jade plant
- kalanchoe
- palms (butterfly, cane, golden feather, Madagascar, European fan, sentry and pygmy date)
- pepperomia
- rubber plant
- spider plant
- yucca

If you have other pets in the home that require flea treatments, consider pyrethrin-based products. These natural flea killers are derived from chrysanthemums and, although they aren't as long-lasting as synthetic substitutes, they do knock down fleas quickly and are safer in the long run. You can also treat your dog or cat's sleeping area with diatomaceous earth, which is the crushed shells of primitive one-celled algae. This dust kills fleas by mechanical means, so fleas will never develop a resistance to it as they could with chemical products.

Interactions between your cockatiel and other family pets should be closely supervised.

OTHER PETS

Other pets can harm your cockatiel's health, too. A curious cat could claw or bite your pet, a dog could step on him accidentally or bite him, or another, larger bird could break his leg or rip off his upper mandible with his beak. If your cockatiel tangles with another pet in your home, contact your avian veterinarian immediately because emergency treatment (for bacterial infection from a puncture wound or shock from being stepped on or suffering a broken bone) may be required to save your bird's life.

If Your Bird Flies Away . . .

One of the most common accidents that befalls bird owners is that a fully flighted bird escapes through an open door or window. Cockatiel owners are at particular risk to lose their birds because cockatiels are so aerodynamic and such strong fliers. Just because your bird has never flown before or shown any interest in leaving his cage doesn't mean that he can't fly or that he won't become disoriented once he's outside. If you don't believe it can happen, just check the lost and found advertisements in your local newspaper for a week. Chances are many more cockatiels turn up in the "lost" column than in the "found" one.

Why do lost birds never come home? Some birds fall victim to predatory animals in the wild, while others join flocks of feral, or wild, parrots (Florida and California are particularly noted for these). Still other lost birds end up so far away from home because they fly wildly and frantically in any direction that the people who find them don't advertise in the same area that the birds were lost in. Finally, some people who find lost birds don't advertise that they've been found because the finders think that whoever was unlucky or uncar-ing enough to lose the bird in the first place doesn't deserve to have him back.

Cockatiels enjoy spending time playing out of their cages.

Prevention

How can you prevent your bird from becoming lost? First, make sure his wings are safely trimmed at regular intervals. Be sure to trim both wings evenly and re-member to trim wings after your bird has molted.

Next, be sure your bird's cage door locks securely and that his cage tray cannot come lose if the cage is knocked over or dropped accidentally. Also be sure that all your window screens fit securely and are free from tears and large holes. Keep all window screens and patio doors closed when your bird is at liberty. Finally, don't ever go outside with your bird on your shoulder.

If, despite your best efforts, your bird should escape, you must act quickly for the best chance of recovering your pet.

Taming Your Cockatiel

If you have acquired a hand-fed cockatiel, chances are that the breeder spent time each day working with your bird to tame it. If that is the case, you must spend time with your bird daily to ensure that his gentle nature and handleability are maintained. If your bird was not tamed before you acquired him, you will have to begin the taming process by gaining your pet's trust, and then working to never lose it. You must also be sure not to lose your temper with your bird and never to hit him, even if the bird makes you very angry.

TRAINING TIPS

- Provide a safe and secure training environment.

- Respect your cockatiel's likes and dislikes.

- Keep sessions short and fun.

- Praise and reward every effort.

Although parrots are clever creatures, they are not "cause and effect" thinkers. If your cockatiel chews on a picture frame on your end table, he won't associate you yelling at him or locking him in his cage with the original mis-behavior. As a result, most traditional forms of disci-pline are ineffective with parrots.

GENTLE DISCIPLINE

So what do you do when your cockatiel misbehaves? When you must discipline your pet, look at him sternly (what bird behaviorist Sally Blanchard calls "the evil eye") and tell him "No" in a firm voice. If the bird is climbing on or chewing something he shouldn't, also remove him from the source of danger and temptation as you tell him "No." If your bird has wound himself up into a screaming banshee, sometimes a little "time out" in his covered cage (between five and ten minutes in most cases) does wonders to calm him down. Once the screaming stops and the bird calms down enough to play quietly, eat or simply move around his cage, the cover comes off to reveal a well-behaved, calmed-down pet.

If your cockatiel bites you while he's perched on your hand or if he begins chewing on your clothing or jewelry, you can often dissuade him from this behavior by rotating your wrist about a quarter turn to simulate a small "earthquake." Your cockatiel will quickly associate the rocking of his "perch" with his misbehavior and will stop biting or chewing.

Keep your arm as stable as possible to help your cockatiel feel safe.

BUILDING TRUST

A good first step in building trust with your cockatiel is getting it to become comfortable around you. To do this, give your bird a bit of warning before you approach his cage. Call his name when you walk into the room. Move slowly around your pet because these gestures will help him become more comfortable with you. Reassure the bird that everything is all right and that he's a wonderful pet.

After your bird is comfortable having you in the same room with him, try placing your hand in his cage as a first step toward taking him out of his cage. Place your hand in your bird's cage and hold it there for a few seconds. Don't be surprised if your bird flutters around and squawks at first at the "intruder."

Continue this process daily, and leave your hand in the cage for slightly longer periods of time each day. Within a few days, your bird won't make a fuss about your hand being in its space, and he may come over to investigate this new perch. Do not remove your hand from the cage the first time your cockatiel lands on it; just let the bird become accustomed to perching on your hand.

After several successful perching attempts on successive days, try to take your hand out of the cage with your bird on it. Some cockatiels will take to this new adventure willingly, while others are reluctant to leave the safety and security of home. (Be sure your bird's wings are clipped and all doors and windows are secured before taking your bird out of his cage.)

IF YOUR COCKATIEL TAKES FLIGHT...

- Have an audiotape of your bird's voice and a portable tape recorder available to lure your bird back home.

- Place your bird's cage in an area when your bird is likely to see it, such as on a deck or patio. Put lots of treats and food on the floor of the cage to tempt your pet back into his home.

- Use another caged bird to attract your cockatiel's attention.

- Alert your avian veterinarian's office that your bird has escaped. Also let the local humane society and other veterinary offices in your area know.

- Post fliers in your neighborhood describing your bird. Offer a reward and include your phone number.

- Don't give up hope.

Once your cockatiel is willing to come out of his cage on your hand, see if you can make perching on your hand a game for your pet. Once he masters perching on your hand, you can teach him to step up by gently pressing your finger up and into the bird's belly. This will cause the bird to step up. As he does so, say "Step up" or "Up." Before long, your bird will respond to this command without much prompting.

Along with the "Up" command, you may want to teach your cockatiel the "Down" command. When you put the bird down on his cage or playgym, simply say "Down" as the bird steps off your hand. These two simple commands offer a great deal of control for you over your bird, because you can say "Up" to put an unruly bird back in his cage or you can tell a parrot that needs to go to bed "Down" as you put the bird in his cage at night.

After your bird has mastered the "Up" and "Down" commands, encourage him to climb a "ladder" by moving it from index finger to index finger (the "rungs"). Keep taming sessions short (about fifteen minutes is the maximum cockatiel attention span) and make the taming process fun because it will be much more enjoyable for both of you.

After your pet has become comfortable sitting on your hand, try petting him. Birds seem to like to have their heads, backs, cheek patches, under wing areas and eye areas (including the closed eyelids) scratched or petted lightly. Quite a few like to have a spot low on their backs at the bases of their tails (over their preen glands) rubbed. Many birds do not enjoy having their stomachs scratched, although yours may think this is heaven! You'll have to experiment to see where your bird likes to be petted. You'll know you're successful if your bird clicks or grinds his beak, pins its eyes or settles onto your hand or into your lap with a completely relaxed, blissful expression on his face.

TRICKS!

Trick training a cockatiel may seem like a daunting task, but it really isn't. You've already trained your pet to perform simple tricks when he learns the "Up" and "Down" commands and to climb the "ladder" that you create with your fingers. You can make further trick training easier by first watching your bird and seeing what he's naturally inclined to do. For example, does your bird spend a lot of time climbing on his ladder or on his rope toys? If he does, make climbing an important part of any tricks you teach your pet. If your bird raises his wings frequently, it may be a good candidate to learn how to salute or "be an eagle."

Birds less than six months of age seem to be easier to teach tricks to than adult cockatiels, and inexperienced trainers may find greater success with younger birds. Regardless of the age of your bird, remember that patience on your part and a cheerful demeanor and attitude will go a long way toward making the training sessions more pleasant for both you and your pet. Your patience will be rewarded by a more enjoyable relationship with your pet bird.

POSITIVE REINFORCEMENT

Another key to trick training success is to use positive reinforcement to reward your bird's good behavior. Bird trainer Steve Martin further breaks down positive reinforcement into primary reinforcers, such as a favorite treat, and secondary reinforcers, such as praise or a scratch on the head. When you first begin training your cockatiel, primary reinforcers will be the reward you want to use. As your bird learns and perfects a trick, you can use secondary reinforcers to reward his behavior.

Some people would tell you that in order to train your bird successfully, you should withhold food from him so that he's hungry. Think how you feel when you're hungry? Do you concentrate well and want to learn new things quickly? I'd imagine that you don't, and your bird is no different. To reward your cockatiel's good behavior, follow trainer Steve Martin's advice and pick one favorite treat, such as half a peanut or a sunflower seed. Use this treat as a reward only during your training sessions and eliminate it from your bird's diet otherwise. In this way, you've modified your bird's diet somewhat to make the treat a special reward without depriving it of food completely.

Keep It Short

The treat can also help you gauge the length of a training session. When your bird has lost interest in this favored treat, end the training session because your bird's lack of interest means you've probably lost his attention for learning the trick as well. If possible, try to end the session before your bird loses interest in the treat because that will allow you to stop the session on a positive note.

How To Get Started

To start trick training your cockatiel, praise him and reward him with a treat when you see the bird doing something—lifting his wing, for instance—that could translate into a trick later on. Your bird will soon associate his actions with attention and positive reinforcement from you, which will make him all the more likely to perform the behavior in the future. Reinforce the behavior with praise and a treat every time you see your bird perform it.

Trick training begins with praise of positive behavior.

After a few sessions of praising the chosen behavior, you should have your bird accustomed to receiving praise for a particular action. Now you can devise a command to prompt the bird into performing the behavior. For example, if you've praised that winglifting bird for raising his wing, you can now cue the bird to "salute." Once you've settled on an appropriate command, praise the bird *only* when he follows your directions. If he doesn't follow your

103

command, don't punish it. Instead, ask him to perform the trick again and praise him when him follows your instructions.

Another easy trick to teach your cockatiel is to shake his head "yes" or "no" as if he's agreeing or disagreeing with you. To do this, show your bird a treat and move it up and down in front of your bird's face to teach him "yes" and from side to side to teach him "no." Praise the bird when he moves his head in the proper direction and give him the treat. Use a phrase like "Do you agree?" as a command or cue when training your bird to nod his head "yes." As you teach this trick, move the treat a little bit further away from your bird with each repetition and wait a bit longer to praise and reward your cockatiel with his treat. Finally, don't teach these tricks simultaneously because you might confuse the cockatiel.

Before you know it, you'll be amazing your friends and family with your trick-trained bird! If, however, your pet doesn't seem to enjoy the training sessions, don't force him into becoming a performer. Instead, appreciate him for the wonderful creature that he is.

TOILET TRAINING

Although some people don't believe it, cockatiels and other parrots can be toilet trained so that they don't defecate on their owners. If you want to toilet train your bird, you will have to choose a command that will indicate the act of defecating to your pet, such as "Go poop" or "Go potty." While you're training your pet to associate the chosen phrase with the action when you see him about to defecate in his cage or on his play-pen, you will have to train yourself to your bird's body language and actions that indicate he is about to defecate, such as shifting around or squatting slightly.

Once your bird seems to associate "Go potty" with defecating, you can try picking him up and holding him until he starts to shift or squat. Tell the bird to "Go potty" while placing him on his cage, where he can defecate. Once he's done, pick him up again and praise him for being such a smart bird! A few accidents can be expected as your bird learns this trick, but soon you'll have a toilet-trained bird that you can put on his cage about every twenty minutes or so.

chapter 8

Your
Winsome
Cockatiel

You've really come to enjoy your pet cockatiel and other cockatiel owners you've met through visits to your favorite bird supply store and your avian veterinarian's office. You want to take the next step—showing your bird—but you're unsure of how to go about it.

Showing Your Cockatiel

First, you need to join a bird club. Attend meetings of your local bird club to see if they have exhibitors who are willing to help people new to showing birds (like you). Go to bird shows as an observer and see which birds win. Talk to the breeders of those birds to see if they have chicks available for purchase. Ask the breeder of your birds, as well as other breeders in the club, to help you start training your birds for the show season, which kicks into high gear in the fall. (We'll discuss conditioning birds for the show circuit shortly, too.)

Once you have some promising show birds, you'll need to know when the show is happening. Bird magazines, club newsletters, and even bulletin boards in pet stores and veterinary offices can be good places to locate this information. Along with the date and location of the event, a contact person's name, address and phone number are usually listed. Call or write this person to obtain a show catalog, which is your guide to the particulars of the show you've chosen to enter. When you make your catalog request, ask again for the date and location of the show, along with the name of the hotel most of the exhibitors will be staying in (this is especially important if you will be traveling to the show, since you'll probably want to make some new friends along the way).

Bird shows are a fun way to show off the unique traits of your cockatiel.

As you read over the show catalog, note the check-in time for your birds (late birds don't have to be accepted for judging) and any entry fees. You will also learn who will be judging your category and what time judging is set to begin, along with what awards will be given out.

The show catalog will also contain information on the divisions, subdivisions, sections and classes that will be judged in this show. Study this information carefully, because you will need to know what information to write down on your show tags and entry forms. Birds that are entered in the wrong classification may be disqualified, so make sure the information you put on your forms is correct.

You will also want to review the written standard for cockatiels, which will be printed in the show catalog, and learn which society is offering points to the show winners.

ABOUT COCKATIEL SOCIETIES

Cockatiels can be shown under the American Cockatiel Society (ACS) standard or the National Cockatiel Society (NCS) standard.

Here the American Cockatiel Society's entrants are being judged at an Orlando, Florida, bird show.

ACS Standard

The ACS was founded in 1976. Its standard calls for a long, graceful bird that is full bodied and well proportioned. The total bird should measure about 17 inches long, with 3 inches given to the bird's crest, which should be long, dense and full, and 14 inches to her large, sleek body and tail.

VISUAL STANDARD

This ideal bird's head should be large and well-rounded with no flat spots and fully feathered. (Bald spots will be penalized.) The bird's eyes should be large and bright, and they should be placed midway between the front and the back of the skull. The bird's brow should be well pronounced and protrude enough to show good distance between the eyes when you see the bird from the front.

The bird's beak should be clean and of normal length. It should tuck in so that part of the lower mandible is visible. The cheek patches should be well-defined, round and bright. Adult males especially will have bright yellow heads with a sharp visual definition of where the yellow feathers meet the body feathers. Deep bibs are preferred and no pinfeathers should be present.

The ACS standard calls for a bird with a relatively long **neck** that has a slight curvature above the shoulder and a small nip above the chest. This gives the bird a graceful silhouette. The bird's **body** should be well muscled with a high, broad chest; a slender abdomen; and a wide, straight back.

This cockatiel has round and vibrant cheek patches that are well defined.

Regarding **wings**, the ACS standard calls for large, wide, long wings that envelop more of the bird's body when you view her from the side. The wings should not cross or droop, and they should be held close to the body. Wing patches should be well defined and clear of dark feathers. All flight feathers should be in place, and the coverts should show their growth pattern clearly.

The bird's **legs and feet** should be able to support the bird. The feet must grasp the perch firmly and they must have all their toes and claws. Finally, the bird's legs and feet should be clean.

The longest feathers of the bird's **tail** should complete an imaginary line that passes straight through the

center of the bird's body. The tail must be carried neither too high nor too low, and all feathers must be
clean, straight and intact.

POINT STANDARD

The ACS supplements this visual standard with a point
standard that awards 60 points to conformation. This
category is further broken into: size (20 points), crest
(10 points), body substance (10 points), proportions
(5 points), wing carriage (5 points), tail (5 points) and
head (5 points). The point standard continues with
15 points for condition, 10 points for deportment,
5 points for caging and 10 points for colors and
markings, which is equally divided between the sub-
categories of uniformity of color and depth of color.

Birds competing for ACS points must be shown in ACS
standard show cages, which measure 17 inches high by
18 inches wide by 10 inches deep. The front of the
show cage is made of a removable chrome grille,
and it contains two 3/4-inch dowel perches that are
placed perpendicular to the cage front. The interior of
the cage is painted a light blue semi-gloss, while the
outside is high-gloss black. While being shown, birds
can have about an inch of seed mixture on the cage
floor and a detachable watering tube.

NCS Standard

The NCS show standard calls for a long, graceful bird
that shows a substantial body. This bird should measure
14 inches from the top of her head to the tip of her tail,
with a crest that is approximately 3 inches in length.
This bird should also be equally proportioned, which
means the measurements from the top of her head to
her vent, from the top of the shoulder to the wing tip
and from the vent to the tip of the tail should be
approximately equal.

VISUAL STANDARD

The ideal bird should have a full, showy **crest** that
curves back gracefully and shows no evidence of a flat
top anywhere along her length.

The NCS standard calls for full, bright **eyes** that are located midway between the front and the back of the bird's skull. The eyes should also be protected by a pronounced brow line, which gives the ideal cockatiel a hawklike appearance from the front.

The bright orange **cheek patches** should be well-colored and well-contained. The male's yellow face should be bright and free of extraneous orange or gray feathers. It should also show a marked contrast from the main body feathers. The bird's **beak** should be of normal length, clean and tucked in, with the lower mandible being only partly visible.

The bird's **neck** should be neither too long nor too short, and it should be evident when the bird is in an alert posture.

When you look at the ideal NCS cockatiel from the front or the rear, she should have good width across her chest and shoulders. The back should be straight and should blend with the slender abdomen. The large, wide **wings** are held tight against the body, and the tips should neither cross nor droop. The bird should have all her flight feathers. The bird should also have an approximately 3/4-inch-wide wing patch that is clear of dark feathers.

THE NATIONAL COCKATIEL SOCIETY

This group which describes itself as the largest cockatiel society in the United States, was founded in 1983. Its members are dedicated to:

- encouraging improvement and enjoyment of the species, whether as a pet, an aviary bird or a show bird

- emphasizing the advantages of selective breeding, close-banding and good recordkeeping

- supporting an annual exhibit of cockatiels at the NCS specialty show

- maintaining a panel of qualified judges who use the NCS standard of excellence

---

The bird's **feet and legs** should be clean and grasp the perch strongly. The bird should also have all her **toes and nails,** and the nails must be trimmed. The tail feathers should be long, clean, straight and complete.

The National Cockatiel Society recognizes normals, cinnamons, pearls, lutinos, pieds, albinos, fallows, silvers and whitefaces in its judging standard.

Looking Good

Now that you have an idea of what the judges are looking for, how do you get your cockatiel to live up to her
own standard of perfection? You train her and groom
her and show her off in a proper show cage.

Show birds must demonstrate grace under pressure
during judging. They must appear calm, but alert, and
comfortable in their show cages (which are likely not
to be their regular cages). They must also be able to
accept and adjust to strangers looking closely at them
and tapping on their cages. Finally, they must be in
perfect feather and tip-top overall condition. Sound
like a tall order? It is, but it can be done!

TRAINING

To train your cockatiel for the show circuit, get her
used to her show cage well before show season starts.
Cockatiel breeder and judge Nancy Reed recommends
that you make your final decisions about show birds at
least two months before the show season begins, so
training should begin at about that time.

About two months before her first show, put the show
cage where your bird can see it. Gradually move the
show cage closer to your bird's home. When your bird
appears curious about, but not frightened of, the show
cage, put your cockatiel in the show cage with the cage
door open. Allow your pet to explore the new cage, but
encourage her to stay on her perch. Your goal is to
train your bird to be as inactive as possible, which isn't
always easy with a cockatiel!

After your cockatiel has learned to stay on the perch,
invite some friends over to simulate a show. Reinforce
your pet's good behavior (staying on its perch and not
showing signs of panic) with praise and a small treat
after "the show."

Next, ask a friend to "judge" your bird. Have this
person get close to the cage and give your cockatiel a
thorough visual inspection. Ask the "judge" to tap
lightly on the show cage with a pointer or pencil and to

poke gently at the bird with this object. Praise your bird for her good behavior. (If, however, your bird seems uncomfortable with this added attention, you may want to reconsider the show circuit for this bird.)

Once you have your bird's training program underway, you'll need to work on her grooming. She will need to be fully feathered (feathers take from three to eight weeks to grow in fully, depending on their size and location on the bird's body), have her wings and nails trimmed and her feet clean to show well. Regular misting with clean, warm water may encourage your bird to preen herself more frequently, which can help improve your bird's appearance if her feathers look a bit rough before a show. If your bird suddenly breaks out in pinfeathers, you may want to reconsider showing her at that time, or you may want to still enter the show as practice.

THE SHOW CAGE

Finally, there's the matter of the show cage. You will need to have a clean cage that is in good shape to show your cockatiel to her best advantage. Again, an experienced exhibitor can help you with this important aspect of showing your bird.

After you've polished your bird's show style, take a little time to work on yours. Start by entering only healthy birds in the show. Next, follow all show rules and maintain a positive attitude throughout the show. Be considerate of staff members and other exhibitors, and stay in designated areas during judging. Finally, be a good loser and an even better winner!

Color Mutations

Color mutations are a popular topic with cockatiel owners. (Breeding questions were the most common inquiries we fielded from cockatiel owners because their birds had taken matters into their own wings and gone to nest.)

In its simplest terms, a mutation is a change. When speaking of cockatiels, mutations refer to dramatic or subtle changes in color or wing marking these little birds have gone through over the years.

A bird's genetic makeup (or genotype) also determines its physical appearance (or phenotype). Birds can have similar outward appearances, yet have different genetic backgrounds. Chromosomes are further subdivided into sex chromosomes (cockatiels inherit one pair of these) and autosomes (the chromosomes that determine all the bird's other characteristics).

This cockatiel family group shows how various mutations occur among individual members.

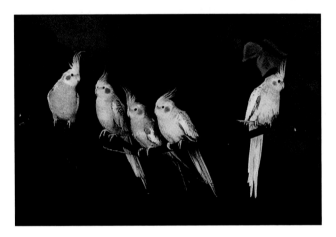

Dominant traits suppress all other traits. These hidden traits may reappear in subsequent generations. Recessive traits show themselves only when two birds that both carry the recessive trait are bred. Otherwise, recessive traits are hidden by dominant traits.

Normal birds are described as homozygous, which means they possess only the genes for the revealed color. Split, or heterozygous, birds carry hidden color traits that may show up in subsequent breedings.

Sex-linked traits are traits that depend on an offspring's gender to appear or disappear. Examples of this type of mutation in cockatiels are the pearl, the cinnamon, the lutino and the albino. The other mutations—pied, silver, white face and fallow—are autosomal recessive, which means that the gene responsible for the mutation is not carried on a sex chromosome.

The last bit of genetic information you need to know before we start our discussion of color mutations is that sex chromosomes in male cockatiels are referred to as ZZ and females are ZY, which differs from the XY used to designate human male chromosomes and XX for human females.

IN THE WILD

In their natural setting, cockatiels are gray birds with yellow crests and faces that are accented by bright orange cheek patches. Males are usually dark gray and have solid-color tails and flight feathers. Females have traces of yellow on their faces, and they have yellow bars on their tails and yellow spots on their flight feathers. From these gray birds came the first cockatiel mutation, pied, in 1949, and mutations are still being developed today. The most recent, yellow face, came about in the early 1980s.

A normal cockatiel.

PIED

The pied was developed in California in 1949. These birds show a combination of white, gray and yellow feathers that can range from resembling a normal gray bird to a bird that has almost no gray feathers on her body.

The ideal pied male is clear (meaning it has no melanin) with brown eyes, gray feet, beak and legs, and his plumage shows irregular white patches. Pied females resemble normal gray females, except that their plumage, too, shows white patches. Females can be split to pied, which means they look like normal birds but produce pied chicks.

Pied cockatiel

115

LUTINO

One of the most popular mutations is the lutino. These whitish-yellow birds were first seen in Florida in 1958, and the mutation resulted from a pair of normal-looking birds. The lutinos were first called "Moonbeams" after the breeder, a Mrs. Moon, who established and popularized the mutation.

Lutino birds lack melanin in their feathers, eyes, beak, feet and nails, which accounts for their light yellow coloring and red eyes. Lutino males are often whiter than females and lack yellow spots on their flight feathers and yellow bars on their tails. The males have red-orange cheek patches, red eyes, pink feet and legs, gray beak and yellow crest. The females' tail bars and wing spots look yellow against a white background in this mutation.

*Lutino cockatiel
(right) with a
pied cockatiel
(left).*

CINNAMON

Cinnamon was developed in Belgium in the late 1960s. Cinnamon birds resemble normal gray birds, except that the black melanin in a normal gray bird has been replaced with brown melanin in the cinnamon bird. The cinnamon's feathers vary from tannish (if they are male) to brownish (if they are female) rather than gray, and their legs and eyes are lighter in color. Chicks hatch with red eyes that darken within a week. This mutation is sometimes referred to as the Isabelle by European breeders.

Although it was first seen in New Zealand in the 1950s, the recessive silver died out there, only to resurface in Europe in the 1960s. The other silver mutation, the dominant silver, was discovered by accident by a breeder who was looking for new stock in a British pet shop in 1979. This bird was eventually bred back to its mother to further the line. Silvers can be described as paler, browner birds than the normal gray cockatiel. Silvers also have black eyes and legs. Male silvers can range in color from smoky brown to silver with the traditional yellow face, while females are dark brown birds.

Cinammon white-faced cockatiel

PEARL

Pearls first appeared in Germany in 1967. This mutation is known for the scalloping that can appear on a bird's breast, wings or back, which is caused by gray feathers that have yellow centers. The eyes of the pearl are black, and its beak, feet and legs are gray.

When this mutation was first developed, pearl males lost their pearl markings after their first molts and looked like normal grays at the age of six months, but breeders in the United States have created pearl males that maintain their pearl plumage into adulthood.

Pure cinnamon pearl cockatiel

WHITE FACE

The white face mutation was first seen in Holland in 1969. As its name implies, white-faced birds have no

117

yellow or orange on their faces. Instead, they resemble black-and-white photographs of normal cockatiels.

FALLOWS

Fallows were developed in Florida in 1971. These red-eyed soft brown birds have been described as being gray-brown by some breeders, while others liken the color to milk chocolate. The most noticeable color change appears on the primary wing feathers of the fallow.

ALBINO

Two existing mutations—the white face and the lutino—were used to develop the albino (which some breeders refer to as the white face/lutino) in Germany in 1980. These pure-white birds have red eyes. They lack not only melanin, but also carotenoid pigments, which is what gives the cockatiel its characteristic cheek patches. Both sexes are completely white with ruby or red eyes.

YELLOW FACE

The most recent mutation to develop is the yellow face. In this mutation, which was introduced in the United States in 1992, the orange cheek patches of the normal gray have been replaced with yellow patches.

Cockatiel breeders can combine the mutations described above into a number of different possibilities. It is possible to breed birds that combine two, three or four mutations.

Caring for Older Birds

If you've offered your cockatiel a varied, healthy diet, taken her to the vet regularly, clipped her wings faithfully and kept her environment clean and interesting, chances are your bird will live into old age. You may notice subtle changes in your bird's appearance and habits as she ages. She may molt more erratically and her feathers may grow in more sparsely as she ages, or she may seem to preen herself less often.

Although little is known about the nutritional requirements of older pet birds, avian veterinarians Branson W. Ritchie and Greg J. Harrison suggest in their book *Avian Medicine: Principles and Applications* (co-authored with Linda R. Harrison) that older pet birds should eat a highly digestible diet that allows a bird to maintain her weight while receiving lower levels of proteins, phosphorus and sodium. They also suggest that this diet contain slightly higher levels of vitamins A, E, B12, thiamin, pyridoxine, zinc, linoleic acid and lysine may help birds cope with the metabolic and digestive changes that come with old age.

WHEN YOUR BIRD DIES

Although birds are relatively long-lived pets, eventually the wonderful relationship between bird and owner ends when the bird dies. While no one has an easy time accepting the death of a beloved pet, children may have more difficulty with the loss than adults. To help your child cope, consider the following suggestions:

Let your child know that it's okay to feel sad about losing your cockatiel. Encourage your child to draw pictures of the bird, to make a collage using photos of your pet or pictures of cockatiels from magazines, to write stories or poems about her or to talk about your loss. Also explain to the child that these sad feelings will pass with time. Regardless of a child's age, being honest about the loss of your bird is the best approach to help all family members cope with the loss.

While helping their children cope with the death of a pet, parents need to remember that it's okay for adults to feel sad, too. Don't diminish your feelings of loss by saying "It's only a bird." Pets fill important roles in our lives and our families. Whenever we lose someone close to us, we grieve. If someone in your family needs to discuss the loss further, the University of California has established a pet loss support hot line. Call (916) 752-4200 for further information. The Delta Society also maintains a directory of pet loss resources. More information about this directory is available by calling (206) 226-7357. Your avian veterinarian's office may know of pet loss support groups in your area, or you may be able to find one by contacting a local animal shelter or SPCA office. Finally, some pet loss support groups are available online through the Internet.

Although you may feel as though you never want another bird because of the pain caused by your bird's death, don't let the loss of your cockatiel keep you from owning other birds. While you can never replace your cockatiel completely, you may find that you miss having a feathered companion around your house. Some people will want a new pet bird almost immediately after suffering a loss, while others will want to wait a few weeks or months before bringing another bird home. Maybe you want another cockatiel, or perhaps you'd like to try owning a different avian species. Discuss bringing home a new pet bird with your family, your avian veterinarian and bird breeders in your area.

part four

Beyond the Basics

chapter 9

Resources

Books

For more information on bird care, look for these at your local library, bookstore or pet store:

Alderton, David. *You and Your Pet Bird.* New York: Alfred A. Knopf, 1994

———. *A Birdkeeper's Guide to Cockatiels.* Tetra Press, 1989.

Bedford, Duke of. *Parrots and Parrot-like Birds.* New Jersey: TFH Publications, Inc., 1969.

Brokmann, Jörgen, and Lantermann, Werner. *The World of Lovebirds.* New Jersey: TFH Publications, Inc., 1990.

Doane, Bonnie. *My Parrot My Friend: An Owner's Guide to Parrot Behavior.* New York: Howell Book House, 1994.

———. *The Parrot in Health and Illness.* New York: Howell Book House, 1991.

Forshaw, Joseph M. *Parrots of the World.* New Jersey: TFH Publications, Inc. By arrangement with Doubleday and Co., Inc., 1977.

Freud, Arthur. *All About Parrots.* New York: Howell Book House, 1980.

———. *The Complete Parrot.* New York: Howell Book House, 1995.

Gallerstein, Gary A., DVM. *The Complete Bird Owner's Handbook*. New York: Howell Book House, 1994.

Lowell, Michele. *Your Pet Bird*. New York: Henry Holt and Company, 1994.

Reed, Nancy A. *Cockatiels! Pets   Breeding   Showing*. New Jersey: TFH Publications Inc., 1990.

Ritchie, Branson W., DVM, PhD, Harrison, Greg J., DVM, Harrison, Linda R. *Avian Medicine: Principles and Application*. Wingers Publishing Inc., 1994.

Vriends, Matthew M., PhD. *The New Cockatiel Handbook*. Barron's Educational Series Inc., 1989.

Wolter, Annette. *Cockatiels: A Complete Pet Owner's Guide*. Barron's Educational Series Inc., 1991.

Magazines

Bird Talk magazine. Monthly magazine devoted to pet bird ownership. Subscription information: P.O. Box 57347, Boulder, CO 80322-7347.

Bird Breeder magazine. Bimonthly magazine dedicated to the concerns of bird breeders who raise and sell pet birds. Subscription information: P.O. Box 420235, Palm Coast, FL 32142-0235.

Birds USA. Annual magazine aimed at first-time bird owners. Look for it in your local bookstore or pet store.

Caged Bird Hobbyist. This magazine for pet bird owners is published seven times a year. Subscription information: 5400 NW 84 Ave., Miami, FL 33166-3333.

Cockatiels YearBOOK. Published by yearBOOKS Inc., 1 TFH Plaza, Neptune, NJ 07753. Look for it in your local pet store or bookstore.

Online Resources

Bird-specific sites have been cropping up regularly on the Internet. These sites offer pet bird owners the opportunity to share stories about their pets, along with trading helpful hints about bird care.

If you belong to an online service, look for the pet site (it's sometimes included in more general topics, such as "Hobbies and Interests," or more specifically "Pets"). If you have Internet access, ask your Web Browser software to search for "cockatiels," "parrots" or "pet birds."

American Animal Hospital Association
http://www.healthypet.com

Association of Avian Veterinarians
AAVCTRLOFC@aol.com

American Veterinary Medical Association
http://www.avma.org/care4pets/

National Cockatiel Society
http://www.upatsix.com/ncs/

Online Pet Cockatiel Questions
http://www.cockatiels.org/ncs/features/
petcare.html

Veterinary Information

Association of Avian Veterinarians
P.O. Box 811720
Boca Raton, FL 33481

Write to this organization for a recommendation of an avian veterinarian in your area.

Bird Clubs

African Parrot Society
P.O. Box 204
Clarinda, IA 51632-2731

American Cockatiel Society
9527 60th Lane North
Pinellas Park, FL 34666

American Federation of Aviculture
Box 56218
Phoenix, AZ 85079-6218

Publishes bimonthly magazine, The Watchbird, *devoted to bird breeding (all species, not only those kept as pets).*

Australian Aviculture
52 Harris Rd.
Elliminyt, Victoria 3249
Australia

Publishes Australian Birdkeeper, *a bimonthly magazine devoted to aviculture.*

Avian Information Management
P.O. Box 369
Felton, CA 95018-0359

Avian Information Management can help you find a bird club in your area.

Avicultural Society of America
P.O. Box 5516
Riverside, CA 92517-5517

Publishes monthly bulletin detailing socoiety's activities.

Bird Clubs of America
P.O. Box 2005
Yorktown, VA 23692

International Avicultural Society
P.O. Box 280383
Memphis, TN 38168

National Cage Bird Show Club, Inc.
25 Janss Rd.
Thousand Oaks, CA 91360

National Cockatiel Society
286 Broad St., Suite 140
Manchester, CT 06040

Publishes monthly magazine.

National Parrot Association
8 N. Hoffman Lane
Hauppage, NY 11788

Society of Parrot Breeders and Exhibitors
P.O. Box 369
Groton, MA 01450

PARROT CONSERVATION ORGANIZATIONS

United States World Parrot Trust
P.O. Box 341141
Memphis, TN 38184

OTHER ORGANIZATIONS

National Animal Poison Control Center Hotline
(800) 548-24231

Parrot Rehabilitation Society
P.O. Box 6202213
San Diego, CA 92612-0213

*The Parrot Rehabilitation Society rescues and rehabilitates
abused and neglected parrots.*